Positive Thinking Mastery:

Boost Your Happiness, Confidence, Self Discipline & Social Skills With 2 Self Help Books In 1 - Stoicism For Beginners & Emotional Intelligence (For Men, Women & Teens)

Table Of Contents

Introduction 2

Chapter One: Stoicism: History and Philosophy 4

Chapter Two: Stoicism: In the Modern World 9

Chapter Three: Know Thyself 15

Chapter Four: The Power of Meditation 21

Chapter Five: Choosing Virtue Ahead of Immorality 26

Chapter Six: Eliminating Emotions 33

Chapter Seven: Being Logical at All Times 39

Chapter Eight: Living a Stress-Free Life 43

Chapter Nine: Beating Depression with Stoicism 48

Chapter Ten: Being Calm Amidst Adversities 54

Chapter Eleven: Indifference: Unveiling the Goodness in You 62

Chapter Twelve: A Pinch of Stoicism in Our Daily Lives 68

Chapter Thirteen: Stoicism: A Pathway to Joy, Happiness, and Positivity 73

Chapter Fourteen

Chapter Fifteen: A New Dawn! 85

Conclusion 95

Introduction 98

Chapter One: What is Emotional Intelligence? (Definitions and Concepts) 100

Chapter Two: Identifying and Improving Emotional Intelligence in Yourself and in Others Around You. 109

Chapter Three: Secrets to Boosting Your Spirituality and Tapping into an Endless Amount of Joy 118

Chapter Four: Proven Emotional Intelligence Strategies to Drive Your Success, Power, and Motivation 126

Chapter Five: How You Can Boost Your Emotional Intelligence Almost Overnight 135

Chapter Six: 7 Tips to Increase Your EQ for Better Relationships 143

Chapter Seven: 19 Ways to Improve Your Emotions in 2019 153

Chapter Eight: The Little-Known Time-Tested Principles to Follow If You Want to Persuade Others 167

Chapter Nine: The Dark Side of Emotional Intelligence 174

Chapter Ten: Does Emotional Intelligence Really Exist? (Now you know better) 181

Conclusion 185

Stoicism for Beginners:

An Empowering Introduction to Stoic Philosophy, Daily Meditations and a Guide to the Art of Joy, Happiness, Positivity, Stress and Life – Be Happy, Stop Anxiety and Beat Depression!

Introduction

When we hear the word "stoicism," "stoics," or even "stolidity," one thing keeps ringing in our head - indifference! Indifference to pain, indifference to pleasure, indifference to our sense of reasoning, and indifference to our raging emotions. Nevertheless, stoicism goes way beyond just Indifference. It encapsulates our very existence.

It is important to know that stoicism as a philosophy started more than a thousand years ago. As a matter of fact, early stoicism dates back to the days of the old Athens, in the Greek setting. Zeno was the father of early stoicism with many scholars and thinkers doting on his philosophy, even after his death.

Many centuries later, the term stoicism became synonymous with thinkers of antiquities such as Kant, Montaigne, Deleuze, and Nietzsche. According to these scholars, the world and humans are two connected but distinct components which should work hand in hand for a better cosmos.

They further believe that the world is materially and secularly inclined with humans playing a role in this formation, especially as a rational animal. However, the rise and introduction of the Modern Stoics saw the regression of the views, tenets, and beliefs of the early Stoics as it contradicts with the true nature and set up of the modern world.

This gave birth to the paradigm shift in some of the core values of the principles of Stoicism. Modern day Stoicism now focus on the acknowledgment of facts ahead of nature, elimination of violent emotions toward much better reasoning, and upholding virtue as the only gateways towards being happy.

In other words, a clear mind devoid of emotions is a perfect mind. Be that as it may, what this book seeks to do is familiarize and enlighten you on the concepts of Stoicism. It also seeks to take you through a stress-free journey of being a better version of what you were yesterday.

A lot of people have made their mistakes from making what could have been a simple problem into a cumbersome one. If only they had added a little bit of logic and emotionless attitude, the problem would have been dealt with accordingly. But most times, we tend to let our emotions take total control of us, thereby making decisions that will leave us unhappy in the end.

This book will equip you with the right mindset toward making a better judgment, even in the face of adversity. It will enlighten you on how to beat depression and anxiety without even trying. Read through the chapters with rapt attention, and I can assure you you'll come out stronger, better, and wiser in making decisions that influence your life.

We all deserve to be happy. We all deserve to lead a good life. Clear your mind and allow us to take you through this breathtaking experience. Happy reading!

Chapter One

Stoicism: History and Philosophy

The old Greek setting has been quite popular for its wonderful and soul-captivating theories, principles, and philosophies, which are still very vital in today's world. Even after these theories, principles, and philosophies had been conceived for over thousands of years, they still remain vital and relevant in today's world, thereby forming the roots of all modern work.

For instance, the great Greek scholars of antiquities like Socrates, Aristotle, and Plato have become tenets and foundations which had given birth to lots of modern works out there. Notwithstanding, it is important to know that philosophies during the old Greek setting feature every aspect and corner of the world in general.

From war to love, nature, science, geography, biology, and so much more. With that being said, our focus will be on one of Greek finest philosophies - Stoicism.

Ancient Stoicism was first started as a movement in the late 300 BCE by the great Zeno of Citium before it gradually graduated into a school of thought. As a movement, the believers of this early philosophy met at the popular "Painter Stao," which is located at the market place of Greece's most populous city, Athens. Little wonder why the school of thought got its name "Stoic."

Unlike the already well-established school of Plato (Academy), Aristotle's school (Lyceum), and the Epicurus school (Garden), which was gaining momentum during that period, Zeno's Stoic movement was just beginning to establish itself as an upcoming, new school of thought. They never had the opportunity and facilities these other schools had.

As a matter of fact, they only met at various public spots situated in the city of Athens. It is important to know that Stoicism started gaining much popularity only after the death of its founder, Zeno of Citium. Little by little, Zeno's student, Cleanthes, carried on with the propagation of his teacher's work.

People of Athens now begin to infuse and inculcate Stoicism in their daily life, thereby giving the school of thought a heavy boost throughout the city.

Stoicism and the Roman Empire

Over the course of time, Rome rose to become the center of power and politics during the first century BCE. Romans had studied the Stoic philosophy and deemed it perfect for their fast-growing nation. The ideologies and principles of Zeno's school of thought became the guiding force toward leading the glorious Rome.

This was evident in the summaries Cicero introduced to the Latin-speaking world on the importance of mastering Stoicism. Afterward, there was a large acceptance and reception of Stoicism all over Rome, and especially in other cities of the world, such as Seneca, Lucan, Perseus, Musonius, Rufus, and Epictetus.

Romans now saw life from a whole new perspective, unlike what the other schools had posited. Stoicism taught them rationality. Stoicism taught them accountability for their actions. Stoicism taught them the real meaning of life. It taught them what was right and wrong.

To this effect, Stoicism encapsulates different core theories ranging from ethics, epistemology, and ontology. It opens up your mind to see the true nature of the world. Nevertheless, before Zeno became inspired by this philosophy, there were chunks of previous philosophies that had laid emphasis on this line of thoughts.

So the question remains, what makes Stoicism stands out? The difference is very clear in the central tenets and focus of the Stoic philosophical system. The Stoics posit that the world is materially inclined. It is driven by a material force which is created by a supernatural being.

It also argued that for us to be eternally happy, we must uphold virtue and morality alone. Material benefits are totally irrelevant in attaining genuine happiness. Furthermore, our emotions shouldn't guide our judgments and deductions. In fact, they are merely a product of our irrationality and should be eliminated.

Stoicism thereby encourages you to be rational, devoid of emotions, and indifferent to events, phenomena, and activities revolving around you. The principle of Stoicism had painted its school of thought around a picture of a perfect man who would only attain true happiness even in the face of torture by upholding morality and virtue, thereby becoming highly rational, emotionless, and indifferent.

Stoicism later grew in followers over time. The loss of major traditional text which points to the early principles of the school of thought led to its high regression in the third century BCE. However, the philosophy started gaining grounds as modern philosophers started building on the origin of the school.

The Cicero Summary which was written in Latin, fragments of the "Painted Stao" gathering written by early authors, and other early works gave credence to the school's postulations. This further boosted their influence in the sixteenth and seventeenth century.

Key Concept of the Philosophy

1. Virtue and Morality: Early Stoics believed that there was more to life than just reckless living. The only way to attain real happiness is via upholding virtue and morality. While many of the schools in the old Greek setting contradict this concept, Stoics believe these two concepts are what we need to live a meaningful life.

They believe morality and virtue define courage, good character, justice, and good traits. Not many people possess these kind of outstanding qualities. Thus, mastering and studying the philosophy of Stoicism is the only way one can truly understand the principles.

To this effect, it is pertinent to know that in order to live a stress-free life, one must not only study the principles of Stoicism academically but also infuse them into our way of life practically.

Stoics also posit that all humans have the tendency and free will to choose from what is right and what is wrong. They have the tendency to follow the path of morality or virtue and not immorality or evil. In other words, we are accountable for every one of our actions, either good or bad.

2.   Emotions: According to Stoics, anyone who can successfully devoid themselves of emotions when making decisions, irrespective of the circumstances, would eventually live a fulfilled life. In other words, he who can eliminate or separate himself from emotions at all times is a complete Stoic.

With that being said, the idea of emotions is not entirely evil to the Stoics. This will be further explained in the next chapter of this book. To this effect, we shouldn't let this be the drive behind our decision making. If we let our emotions take the better part of us, we might end up not making a very smart move.

Thus, a rational way of making a decision is the best way we can follow in coming up with logical solutions to our problems. The sweet feeling that comes with making the right decision is the only true and appropriate emotion we should feel.

So don't get it twisted, Stoics are actually in support of emotions. Emotions are feelings we can't do without. But they should be sidelined and differentiated from the important aspects of human existence (decision making, judgments, living a good life, and maintaining nature).

3.   Harmonic Co-existence: This is one great concept about Stoicism. Irrespective of our principles, ideologies, and way of life, we shouldn't cease to co-exist in peace and harmony. This can only be achieved via our strive toward a logical existence. According to the words of Marcus Aurelius in his Meditations,

"We were born for cooperation, like feet, like hands, like eyelids, like the rows of upper and lower teeth. So to work in opposition to one another is against nature: and anger or rejection is opposition."

Stoicism focuses on the connection between man and nature. They both are a part of the whole. Thus, they should work together in harmony. In other words, living a careful and stress-free life, putting nature first, and maintaining our environment.

Want to be a Stoic? It's very simple! All you need to do is to master the principles and tenets. Stoicism as a philosophy has helped a lot of people become truly happy. It has helped rise nations and organizations. Practice Stoicism every day of your life and watch yourself move from leading a normal life to living a happy life. However, the face of Stoicism changed in the new world as there is a paradigm shift in its concepts and ideas.

This and more is what we will discuss in the next chapter. You wouldn't want to miss it.

Chapter Two

Stoicism: In the Modern World

The late 20th century and the early 21st century ushered in the beginning of a new era of Stoicism. The world today has taken a whole new dimension with the presence of many diverse schools of thought in stiff competition with the Stoic philosophy. Nevertheless, Stoicism in the modern world covers the efforts, infusion, and inculcation of Stoic beliefs with the present state of nature.

Therefore, it is important to note that the early tenets of this school cannot be originally applied without tweaking and making the necessary adjustments to suit the current state of the world.

Like we know, the world itself entails changing phases and events. A lot has changed from the first century to the present century. Philosophies have evolved, new inventions are pioneered, and ideas are refurbished. To this effect, old Stoicism can also be said to have passed through the process of reformation and transformation, so as to blend in with the present world.

These blended ideas and movement are what is called Modern Stoicism. Modern Stoicism regained quite a bit of recognition all over the world in November 2012 after the successful event of the First Annual Stoic Week which took place at Exeter University in England. According to statistics, the blogs got numerous hits, over 150 people signed up to the Stoic Week page every week, and notable newspapers like the Guardian and the Independent also graced pages of their newspapers with articles on the event.

Ever since then, the idea of living like a Stoic has been well received, especially with the way people now live their lives with less importance. They now begin to see Stoicism in a different light as it enlightens them on how to really live one's life with absolute contentment.

Virtue and morality theme the arguments of all Modern Stoics. For example, the notable and scholarly works of Alasdair MacIntyre and Philippa Foot have laid emphasis on the need for virtue and morality, which in turn signals the presence of Stoicism. Even in the early Stoic principles, virtue and morality championed their arguments.

One man all Modern Stoics can claim to have drawn their ideas and formed their roots from is none other than Lawrence Becker. In Becker's major Stoicism work named "A New Stoicism", which was published in 1997, he writes,

"It is interesting to try to imagine what might have happened if Stoicism had had a continuous twenty-three hundred year history; if Stoics had had to confront Bacon and Descartes, Newton and Locke, Hobbes and Bentham, Hume and Kant, Darwin and Marx."

Following the above quote of Lawrence Becker, you would agree with me that the early tenets, beliefs, and principles had to be brushed up so as to fit the present statuesque. However, brushing up doesn't necessarily mean that the philosophy has lost its core values. As a matter of fact, it still remains the same, but with a much better approach and view of the world.

Modern Stoic Philosophy

There has been a divide in the philosophical beliefs of Modern Stoicism. Logic, Physics, and Ethics are the three notable elements that make up Ancient Stoic beliefs. However, a lot of Modern Stoic scholars have argued that the latter (Ethics) alone holds up the tenets of Stoicism with Logic and Physics adding little or no value to the already laid principles.

In the same vein, other Modern Stoic scholars believe this notion is outright wrong. In fact, the old Stoics innovated the tenets and beliefs of Stoicism around these three topoi (core areas); Physics, Logic, and Ethics, for a reason.

Physics encapsulates other core areas such as science, theology, and metaphysics. These areas help us gain a better understanding of the modern world as a material cosmos. Ethics, on the other hand, goes way beyond what is right and what is wrong. It entails how to lead a good life, how to be genuinely happy, and so much more.

Logic covers more ground than just the formal logic outlook other scholars tend to attach to it. It goes way beyond that. It touches informal logic down to rhetoric, psychology, and cognitive science.

Stoicism all points to deriving true happiness from living a good life. How about making rational and logical conclusions and decisions to lead a good life? How about understanding nature, so as to be able to make good and rational decisions? You can see they are all connected, right? Ethics go hand in hand with Logic and Physics in order to master Stoicism.

Modern Stoicism as a Movement

The Modern Stoicism movement is a global phenomenon. Nevertheless, the world is globally in sync, with ICT holding the strong chain that binds every part of it together. When we say ICT, we are referring to social media and online activities. To this effect, the propagation of Modern Stoicism has relied heavily on the use of mass media and online platforms.

The First Annual Stoic Week held at Exeter University in England gave popularity to the movement as it was heavily broadcasted online, in blogs, and in newspapers. In 1996, another important online platform was created (The New Stao) and has been able to reach millions of people over the last two decades.

Podcasts also gave credence to the movement. The Sunday Stoic and The Practical Stoic podcasts are examples of the many podcasts that sprung up, gaining interests from people from all over the world.

Internet had no doubt provided Stoics with a brand new way to preach their gospel to anyone that cared to listen. From blogs to newspapers, podcasts, social media (Facebook, Twitter, etc.), and any other internet gateways.

Aside from the internet, there has been an increase in the number of meet-ups, conventions, events, and workshops in places like Helsinki, Denver, London, San Francisco, Warsaw, Australia, Manchester, Milwaukee, Dublin, and many more.

Modern stoics are synonymous with beliefs that there should be a change in the society as regards economic slump, gender discrimination, immortality and evil, environmental treatment, material consumption, reckless living, accountability for our decisions and actions taken, and so much more.

Notable Key Concepts

1.   Virtue, Agency, and Happiness: Modern Stoics like Lawrence Becker believe that virtue, agency, and happiness go hand in hand. In other words, the call for virtue can only be perfected through the right organization of agencies, which in turn would lead to true happiness.

One who has a great amount of control and stability over his or herself is bound to be happy in the long run - even if not immediately. The agency in this view is understood to be our being or self. If we uphold the necessary virtues and exert them on our decisions and judgments, we will surely end up being happier than we have ever been.

2. Nature: Even the Ancient Stoics believed in the maintenance of nature. Thus, in order to lead a life of virtue and be truly happy, nature must be maintained and cherished. They also posited that nature is inherently good and the purpose of its creation is toward a good end.

Therefore, if we follow nature, we will surely end up being good. Nevertheless, the Ancient Stoics' view of nature cannot be applied or can be very difficult in its application to the modern world, especially with the way everything is being configured by science and technology.

Now, the following of nature can be quite wrong, especially with the rate of genocide, atrocities, and evil the modern world is characterized by. If this old Stoic belief is followed, one might be completely out of bounds. Thus, seeing nature as inherently good doesn't hold much substance.

Many Modern Stoics like Lawrence Becker have given their opinions on this concept of "following nature." According to their assumption, Stoicism would have been perfect without the "following nature" concept. But the bad news is that the concept had been synonymous with Stoicism for far too long. Thus, eliminating this concept would mean eliminating an important part of Stoicism.

To this effect, a reinterpretation of the concept became the next best thing to do by this group of Modern Stoics. They believed that instead of following nature blindly like the traditional Stoics, facts about nature should be followed instead. Now the question remains, what does "following facts" mean?

Simply put, following facts means getting the necessary facts about events, phenomena, and circumstances that surround us before making conclusions and judgments. That way, we will end up achieving true happiness.

3.   Ascetic and Renunciation: Stoicism tenets focus on the indifference to both the pains and pleasures of our lives. According to early Stoics, attaining this indifference would make you a complete Stoic. In other words, differentiating your emotions from your reasoning and judgment is key.

However, there is no generally acceptable unit used in measuring ascetic elements oer defining the pleasures and pains of life. Nevertheless, we shouldn't mistake Stoicism for Asceticism. They are both completely different things.

First of all, Stoicism believes true happiness can only be attained when people reach eudemonia - and not from the ordinary material pleasures life would offer you. A stoic is not a monk. Stoicism goes beyond living an ascetic life. As a matter of fact, Stoicism entails accepting nature along with its goodness, lushness, diversity, and sensuality.

Little wonder why lots of people today now see the true meaning of existence. It goes beyond getting that esteemed college degree. It goes beyond having a perfect family. It also goes beyond getting a six-figure monthly salary. Being truly happy while fulfilling the true meaning of life is what our consequent chapters will discuss. But before then, one really needs to understand oneself in order to know which steps to take toward being a true Stoic.

Now, the question remains, how well do you know yourself? Want to find out? Then flip the page over.

Chapter Three

Know Thyself

One of the greatest and shortest quotes ever said by an ancient Greek philosopher (Socrates) is "Know Thyself." These can be said to be the words of a dying man before facing persecution by his Greek lords and authorities. With these simple words, he has challenged even the dumbest of us into checking ourselves to see if we truly know our own selves.

Today, knowing ourselves is the first step one must take before reformation, transformation, and refurbishment. Sometimes, we might have made decisions that do not favor us in the long run. We obviously won't know this at first because our sense of reasoning or judgment might have been influenced by emotions.

But after some time, we start seeing things clearly. Questions now begin to run through our minds. Questions like: Are we making the best decisions for ourselves? Is this truly what we deserve? What would we have done if given a second chance?

Knowing oneself is what pushed the Zeno of Citium into giving birth to this philosophy in the first place. A brief study into his life would enlighten you on the importance of knowing oneself and knowing what is right from what is wrong in order to live a glorious and happy life.

Zeno of Citium was a sailing merchant who had spent more than half of his life inside the confines of a ship. He had derived joy in making ends meet with this line of trade and it was working very well for him. Now, imagine how one would have easily thought of a sailing merchant transforming into one of the founders of the Greek school of thoughts. Quite crazy, right?

Well, it's pretty easy. Some events and circumstances in life end up unlocking a part of us we never knew existed, making us see life in a clearer view. This same thing happened to Zeno of Citium. But in his case, an unforgettable experience. A shipwreck changed the next chapters of his life.

This change of events in his life opened up a new path he sought out. It made him go through the sober reflection phase, which shone lights on a certain aspect of his life that he had neglected. This made him understand himself even better. The shipwreck that almost claimed his life spurred up something in him – the hope and desire to lead a good and happy life.

Now let's ask ourselves this question: Has any event, circumstance, or happening revolving around us spurred up the real us? It is important to know that after Zeno of Citium knew himself better, things changed for him. A new light shone on a new path which he followed. Only then, he became really happy, wise, and articulate.

He knew the solution to the unhappiness of people around him, the solution to the stressful life people around him led, the solution to the atrocities and evil people around him portrayed. He also knew sentiments and emotions do more harm than good. They will never get anybody anywhere. Thus, he founded Stoicism.

Aside Zeno of Citium, a lot of other scholars of this school of thought have also made their mark and contribution towards the development of the philosophy. They have also followed the philosophy of knowing oneself. There is no greater joy than knowing exactly what you want and how to go about achieving it.

Don't get it twisted, people might not buy your idea or even like what you want to begin with. They may criticize and oppose you any opportunity they get. You won't let that deter you from achieving your aims, will you? Your happiness should definitely matter ahead of what others feel or think about your opinion.

Bill Gates didn't get where he is now as a result of letting people's opinions get to him. As a matter of fact, Bill Gates dropped out of college after knowing what he wanted at that particular time. When others were busy bagging their degrees, he was busy turning himself into a better version of what he was. He was busy doing what made him happy.

Don't get me wrong - getting a degree is great, if not superb. But knowing yourself, knowing what you want, and aiming for those things is what will bring you complete happiness. Everyone has his or her own drive. Know yours and happiness would surely be yours.

Now, imagine if Bill Gates had decided not to follow his dreams, his wants, and his path, would he have been truly happy? The answer is no. I'm sure no one would even be able to picture Bill Gates without Microsoft.

It is important to know that knowing oneself is the first step toward being a Stoic. Knowing oneself points to only one thing - coming to terms with being extremely happy by following the dictations of your mind, your desires, your dreams, and your aspirations. These wants end up contributing to the further development of humanity, which is one of the guiding principles of being a Stoic.

A Stoic upholds and maintains the relationship between man and nature. And in order for you to achieve these dreams and goals, your decisions and judgments must be devoid of emotions and sentiments. These and more are the core attributes of a true Stoic.

Just like Zeno of Citium, knowing oneself to be a Stoic is just one step. Familiarizing yourself with the philosophy and practicing it is another step entirely. After the shipwreck which opened a new path for Zeno of Citium, he developed an urge to learn about Greek philosophies, therefore visiting famous books stores in Athens as he embarked on his quest to quench his thirst for knowledge.

He knew he had to seek out books and records of other notable Greek philosophers, so as to get a grip on the basics of all Greek philosophies. Therefore, through your research and findings on Stoicism, I'm sure you will be able to understand yourself even better. Additionally, being a true Stoic comes with being accountable for your decisions and actions.

Before setting out your plans, be sure to be accountable for every action taken. Stoicism will give definition to your life. Instead of living a life of immorality, Stoicism wikk teach you virtue, compassion, humility, and moderation.

Steps to Knowing Oneself

1. Connect to Your Inner Self: This is the first step to knowing yourself. Reaching your inner chakra can be accomplished a lot of ways. Some people may prefer yoga, while others just want to have a nice cool, quiet place where they can think. Be that as it may, we would recommend you record or write down your every thought.

Keep a journal, if possible so that all your thoughts are compiled in a safe place. In the long run, it would surely serve you well as you would be able to revise and go back to the ideas, dreams, and aspirations written or recorded.

Writing in a journal while connecting to your inner self helps you focus and keep your mind afloat from different thoughts and stress. In the end, you will be able to understand, comprehend, and know yourself even better. Connecting to your inner self will clarify your thoughts. It will separate that which is important from which is irrelevant.

2. **Sober Reflection:** Sometimes, when we end up making a wrong move or decision, sober reflection becomes the next best thing to do. Go back to the point where it all began. Then imagine what you would do if the situation presented itself again.

Sober Reflection can only take effect when you retire in solitude. Keep yourself in a quiet place devoid of noise of any kind. That will help you focus on replaying your life over and over again. Rest assured, this process will only make you a better version of yourself.

Your relationship will improve with everyone around you. Sober Reflection sheds light on the path to becoming a better person. It gives you the opportunity to know yourself even better.

3. **Set Standards:** Our core beliefs, principles, and standards are what differentiate us from everybody else. It's what differentiates nations, organizations, and entities. So, therefore, know your standards, so as to set standards that are convenient to you alone. Keep and stick to them no matter what.

Knowing yourself comes with setting your life according to your own terms and standards. These standards ensure that you don't live your life recklessly. As a matter of fact, they are the guiding mechanisms that check our decisions, actions, reactions, and judgments in ensuring we don't live outside our own convenience.

4. **Take Responsibility for Your Actions:** Knowing yourself toward living a happy life comes with honesty and responsibility. No matter what, always be accountable for your actions - no matter how shallow or irrational they may be. Your life is in your hands, thus you should know how to tell what is right from what is wrong.

Don't forget you have a journal that consists of all your strengths and weaknesses. Try to visit this journal from time to time. Know what is right from what is wrong, know your strengths from your weaknesses, and focus on what will make you a better version of yourself.

5. Know What Motivates You: Finding our life purposes can be easier than we had imagined. Motivation differs from person to person. Like the saying goes, "One man's meat is another man's poison." So ask yourself, what motivates you? What do you think can spur up inspiration in you?

6. Weigh Your Relationships: Check your circle. How well do you support one another? How well does your circle help project your true self? These are questions we should ask ourselves when weighing our circle. A relationship is meant to help us to be our very best.

If your circle doesn't include or possess this attribute, then we suggest you start changing it. Most times, the right relationships show us where our problems lie. They nurture and nourish us into becoming our true selves. Thus, we need to handle our relationships with great importance. Those in our world end up becoming the mirrors that reflect our true selves.

Knowing thyself is the key to real happiness. It is the first step to take in preparing your mind. What do you really think you are capable of holding? Are you really willing to let go of your emotions? Is this really what you want? These and more are the questions we should ask ourselves.

No one can tell us about ourselves the way we understand it. Know your self and what you want first - and the best way of doing that is to go into meditation. Want to know how? Then read through our next chapter, as we will walk you through the conversation on how meditation will bring out the real you as well as pave the way for more happiness in your life.

Chapter Four

The Power of Meditation

One of the powerhouses of this school of thought, Marcus Aurelius, has given a lot of insight on the positive effect of meditation toward achieving true happiness. According to his words in his popular book *Meditation*,

"The art of true living in this world is more like a wrestler's, than a dancer's practice. For in this they both agree, to teach a man whatsoever falls upon him, that he may be ready for it, and that nothing may cast him down."

It is important to know that Marcus Aurelius was the Roman Emperor between 161 to 180 AD, and during this period, Rome faced a lot of adversities and hardships. As a Stoic philosopher, meditation became the only way he could reflect on his life. Meditation also became the only way he could seek solutions to the current events disturbing Rome.

As portrayed in the popular movie *Gladiator*, Marcus Aurelius was presented as a good man who faced lots of tribulations and atrocities: Invasion from the borders, internal revolt and coup, and so much more. This is very correct. However, the movie's final scene, showing Marcus Aurelius son murder him is not correct. In reality, Marcus died of smallpox.

Imagine you are a young, open-minded, outright good fellow with lots of betrayers in your circle, who would you trust? What would you do? This is the exact situation Marcus Aurelius faced in his reign as the Emperor of Rome.

He had no one to turn to, so he turned to himself. Meditation gave him a clear head. It helped him continue to stay on the path of righteousness, irrespective of the situations, circumstances, and events revolving around him. That is the power meditation holds.

Be like Marcus Aurelius. Whenever you are faced with issues that may cause an obstacle to your Stoic beliefs and principles, go into that meditation Marcus did, and make sure you come out as a better version of what you were before. Nothing should stop you from reaching your dreams - and in the end, becoming very happy.

You can also write down your meditations just like Marcus Aurelius. These written meditations of Marcus Aurelius have contributed to the Modern Stoic sources of the philosophy. His meditations have helped lay the foundations of Modern Stoicism. The meditation is divided into 12 books and each represents a specific period of time in the life of Marcus Aurelius.

Many Modern scholars believe that Marcus Aurelius meditation was written solely for his own benefit. However, it remains the foundation that holds the Stoic philosophy together. It is simple to comprehend, highly conversational, and easy to read by just anybody.

Meditation and happiness can be said to be two sides of the same coin. The practice goes a long way in moving us from being stressed to being serene. One way or another, it works like magic. Sometimes, we just end up being stressed out. We might even reach a point where giving up would seem like the only option left for us to choose. But have we tried meditation? Just a few minutes of meditation can wash away hours of stress and anxiety.

What meditation does is to refocus your energy into something positive. That way, your energy will be redirected and you will be filled with positivity afterward. According to research, people feel happier after a few minutes of meditation.

As a matter of fact, they stand more upright. They begin to smile more often. They also start accepting themselves with joy concerning how they look, how they sound, how they walk, how they keep their relationships, and even how they coexist with everyone around them.

Marcus Aurelius hit an iceberg of tribulations during his reign as the Roman Emperor. Yet, he was determined to be happy and live a good life. Thus, he started meditating. The happiness that comes out of meditation is real. It lasts longer because of the redirected energy in us.

Don't get it twisted, other happiness boosters like going on vacation, going on a shopping spree, going to a mind-blowing event, spending time with family, and so much more are also great. But the question is - how long do they really last? They wear off as fast as you can imagine, leaving you with the same awful feelings you'd felt before, over and over again.

Additionally, meditation comes quite cheap. You can be in the confines of your room and still meditate. It will only take a few minutes or even hours of your time, depending on the amount of free time you on your hands. We would like you to consider it as the price you'd get to pay for keeping the glow it will give to your face afterward.

There is no measure of the amount of happiness meditation will offer you. Even in the midst of atrocities and tribulations, it kept Marcus Aurelius really happy. Instead of breaking down, it helped him grow stronger in his Stoic beliefs and principles. With meditation, there are no expectations you won't be able to meet, no hurdle you won't be able to cross over, and no obstacle you will not be able to overcome.

Nevertheless, some people are just naturally happy, irrespective of where life places them. But this population is very small in today's world as a majority of us are always grumpy, sad, and unhappy. This is not because we don't have or possess the material benefits to bring us temporary happiness, but because we lack what it takes to be genuinely happy.

Like we said in the previous chapters, no one is a true Stoic until he or she reaches the stage of eudemonia. How can we reach this stage? It's pretty simple. Meditation is one of the gateways to reaching Eudemonia. Little wonder why meditation is now taken seriously by people in the 21st century.

As a matter of fact, a major Information Technology company in Detroit, Michigan made their employees go through a 60 minutes meditation session within the span of seven weeks - and the result was simply overwhelming. There was an immense increase in the focus, emotions, and energy of the employees toward work.

This, in turn, increases the output (i.e. Mindfulness, zeal toward work, decreased illness, increased friendliness, relaxed the tensed working atmosphere, etc.). This is the power of meditation. It makes your goals and purposes in life become much clearer while giving you a clear mind to pursue those goals into reality.

How to Meditate

Meditation is not as hard as people or the media advertises it to be. Notwithstanding, it goes beyond just sitting on a mat wearing fancy pants. It involves concentration. It involves reaching your inner self.

To begin with, finding the perfect place for meditation is vital. You just can't go out there and spread your mat all in the name of meditation. What if it's noisy? What if it's a busy environment? What if it's cold? What if it's hot? These are the questions we should ask ourselves. Get a nice, quiet, comfortable environment or space.

After getting the perfect spot, spread your meditation mat, or cushion as the case may be, and sit or lie comfortably. Be sure to be very comfortable in your sitting style or lying techniques. We wouldn't want a situation where our back, thighs, or even joints might end up hurting at the end of our meditation.

Then closing our eyes and refocusing our mind is the next thing to do. This should force out any negative thoughts that have been going through our minds so as to give us a clear mind in the end. One mistake people make is to start controlling their breathing. This is a mistake. Instead, breathe naturally. Do not breathe heavily, but instead lightly.

Focus on your breathing pace. It is very important to maintain your concentration. And in any case, when your mind wanders off, let your breathing draw you back to your meditation. If you feel numb or tired, you can change your sitting or lying postures - but make sure to maintain concentration.

Do this for as long as you can and you will definitely feel refreshed and renewed. Meditation provides answers to questions we can't seem to find answers to, especially when the outside world is not helping. Tired of seeking advice from people who are not even worth a listening ear? Then look inward and concentrate on your inner citadel with meditation. The answers you need are right there.

But the question remains, do you have the courage to follow it? Read on to the next chapter as we enlighten you on one of Stoics' key principles - Virtue.

Chapter Five

Choosing Virtue Ahead of Immorality

Following what we have discussed in the previous chapters, we have come to understand that one of the key concepts of Stoicism is Virtue and Morality. Stoicism, according to its proponents, scholars, and practitioners, believes that true happiness can be achieved by choosing virtue and morality over sin, reckless living, and immorality. In order words, choosing good over evil in our daily life is the only way a person can achieve true happiness

But rest assured, virtue is part of what we exude almost every day of our lives. Being good to your next door neighbor is a virtue. Helping an old woman cross a busy road is a virtue. As a matter of fact, anything good is a virtue. Thus, the Stoics didn't go wrong when they laid emphasis on being good.

What is Virtue?

Virtue is defined by Stoics as the knowledge of living life the best way - a way that revolves around all aspects of life including personal and business. Furthermore, virtue is a disposition or state where one is considered to be praiseworthy or good. There are four main cardinals that define this state called virtue. It is safe to say these four cardinals are used to analyze the concept of virtue.

The Four Cardinals of Virtue

The four cardinals of virtue are considered as a means of creating an outline to the main events, experiences, and expertise surrounding human life. Stoic theorists believe that the successful combination and infusion of these four cardinals into our existence is the only way one can live a virtuous and fulfilled life.

If one possesses these four characters, according to Stoicism, the person is referred to as a good and a virtuous person. These four cardinals of virtue are as follows:

1. Wisdom (Sophia): Wisdom, or Sophia as referred to in the Greek language, has to do with knowledge and understanding. It is insight, common sense, experience, prudence, and knowledge. This cardinal of virtue is the most general and most important of all the four cardinals. Wisdom here has to do with grasping of knowledge of the good, the bad and the indifferent in life and humanity.

It goes further to emphasize understanding the core value of things and rationally acting upon these values. In other words, wisdom is knowing how to act and understanding what to do in a different situation.

To Stoics, wisdom means understanding and knowing the nature of good. That is, understanding wisdom and living accordingly is true good and a path to happiness. Early Stoic proponents and scholars already laid a firm background to the explanation of wisdom or prudence.

Marcus explained wisdom as the ability to respond to things "in accord with value".

According to Diogenes Laertius, who referred to Chrysippus and others, wisdom or prudence is classified into good counsel (euboulia) and understanding (sunesis).

Stobaeus also said that early Stoics explained wisdom to be the knowing of good and bad, understanding indifference, and knowing the "appropriate action" to take in every situation. It is clear that the Stoics believe that being wise is equal to good.

2. Courage (Andreia): Courage, or Andreia, according to Stoics is a disposition of the mind that is unmoved by fear. It is self-restraint of the soul in situations that are fearful and terrible. Courage is the ability to face intimidation, uncertainty, pain, danger, and agony head on.

In order words, Stoics explain courage as knowing what to do, how to feel, and how to act when faced with adversity and fear in situations of danger like death and other disasters. Diogenes Laertius refers to the classification of courage into two parts by early proponents, which are determination (apparallaxia) and tension (eutonia).

Stobaeus also refer to courage as knowing and understanding what is terrible, what is not terrible, and what is neither (unmoved). Senaca observed that without some traces of fear, virtue cannot exist, because every single person, no matter how perfect or virtuous, needs a little courage.

With the above definitions and explanations, we can come to the conclusion that courage is endurance guided by wisdom.

3. **Self-Control (Sophrosune):** This cardinal of virtue has to do with self-control, temperance, and moderation. This virtue focuses on moderating the soul's pleasures and desires and the ability to discipline one's self when facing desires and pleasures. This is a state or disposition which deals with cautiousness or mindfulness. Modern Christianity is said to have gotten the idea of moral conscience from the virtue of moderation.

This virtue can be defined or analyzed as self-discipline or self-control with self-awareness and self-possession. It is our impulse that guides our reactions and intentions on different desires. Moderation as a virtue is directly opposite to the vice wantonness.

Stobaeus explained moderation here as what is to chosen, avoided and neither. Diogenes Laerteus says the early Stoics defined moderation basically as good discipline. They also subdivided this virtue of moderation into propriety (eutaxia) and decorum (kosmistes). In other words, having the rationale to choose the right thing over one's heart; a desire and pleasure is a form of being virtuous.

4. Justice/Morality (dikaiosune): This good virtue is simply the good discipline of the soul with respect and concern to one another. Justice is goodwill to others, kindness, and benevolence. It is the state or disposition where one chooses what is just. This is a situation of choosing a law-abiding path to life and social equality. This is simply obeying the laws already in place.

In Stoicism, justice doesn't only mean being just in the legal sense. It also has to do with being just in the moral sense, not only in our personal dealings but in our dealings with others and humanity in general. In the early years of Stoicism, its scholars and practitioners referred to this virtue as righteousness, but in modern times it is safe to define this virtue as morality. The direct vice to this virtue is being unjust or morally doing wrong by another person.

In order words, justice can be viewed as prudence applied to our actions. Stobaeus defined justice as understanding and the knowledge of distributing fair value to everyone. According to Diogenes Laertius, Stoics subdivided justice into impartiality (isotes) and kindness (eugnomosune).

Immorality

Immorality is equal to a violation of moral laws, moral standards, and moral norms. It is a state or disposition of badness and wickedness. Stoics believe that immorality is the highest form of vice which is the direct opposite of virtue and should be stayed away from in order to achieve full happiness and live a fulfilled life.

Immorality is shunned upon by Stoics, and this philosophy preaches choosing virtue ahead of immorality and sin. The concept of immorality is considered to be as a result of ignorance. They believe that only reasoned choices are moral and evil choices are not the best of choice. That is to say, a person who does evil or wrong does not understand a better way.

Though immorality is far from accepted in Stoicism, this philosophy accepts and acts in the interest of their neighbors and humanity at large no matter how immoral they are.

Choosing Virtue Ahead of Immorality

Having explained what Stoics believe virtue and immorality are, it is up to us as human beings to choose which is preferable and better for us and humanity in general.

Choosing virtue over immorality is certainly the ultimate path to achieving happiness or eudemonia according to the Stoics. Virtue in this sense is very necessary and sufficient for happiness, that is to say, virtue (wisdom, justice, self-control, and courage) is all you need to be happy and for you lead a happy life.

Choosing virtue ahead of immorality also gives us the idea that the concept of virtue (the only true good) creates a firm basis for strategic thinking and decision making in any given scenario. This has to do with patiently reflecting on the particular situation and properly using a form of virtue to respond to the situation. This goes to say, virtue helps us decide a proper way of reacting to different situations with truthfulness, gentleness, wisdom, and courage.

Virtue also creates a form of acceptance in our lives as human beings. With the idea of virtue in mind, one is likely to accept all the trial of life as they come our way. The situation where one can't accept the trials they face is what leads to sadness, depression, anger, and heartbreak, which are the order of today.

In essence, choosing virtue ahead of morality gives us the ability to control our desires and fears with wisdom, hence creating a lifestyle devoid of sadness and pain - in other words, happiness.

Choosing virtue ahead of immorality helps us focus on the generality of humanity and everyone we come in contact with. With the ideology of kinship and familiarity at heart, Stoics are just in their actions and, this in most cases provides a better way to act in a given situation. If Stoicism is embraced by humanity and virtuous act are chosen over immoral acts, compassion will be the order of the day as Stoicism encourages the idea of compassion.

Immorality, on the other hand, is generally associated with evil, badness, and wickedness. Now, in the law of the universe, you get what you give - or in other words, you reap what you sow. Therefore, in this situation, if you sow evil, wickedness, and badness, you will likely reap any of those.

This goes to show you that the choice of immorality only leads to pain, badness and sadness - not happiness. This is another reason to choose virtue ahead of immorality.

Going further, many modern-day analysts and scholars believe that Stoicism is the best choice of philosophy that should be practiced by humanity in a world where there are many terrible vices and in a world where lives are being lost daily. This philosophy is highly recommended because of its teachings of oneness and virtue.

Following the teachings of Marcus Aurelius, it is safe to come to the conclusion that Stoicism is the best option for the state of our world today. These teachings emphasize treating all humans as family, with his belief that error in judgments is not an intentional act. He further teaches that a Stoic cannot be hurt by others; they can only hurt themselves through a vicious response.

Stoicism promotes the belief that everyone can develop virtue as virtues are not dependent on inborn qualities, background, or intellectual education. It is believed that every human being possesses an innate quality that lets us separate the good from the bad/evil. This quality can only be developed. Development in itself is a virtuous act. They further stress that the general idea of development and the major role of development is a life-long journey, not just a transition into adulthood.

To top it all, the similarity we all have as human beings is the ability to embark on a journey to gain progress. This journey can also be said to be a journey of virtue. It is important to also note that this ancient philosophy of Stoicism has positively impacted many modern ideologies and theories about ethics. It also provides an alternative system for guidance in life.

Flip through the next pages as we continue to help you on your quest to be happy.

Chapter Six

Eliminating Emotions

It is important to note that the popular notion that Stoics are emotionless cows standing under the rain is a totally false statement or notion. Having the ability to control one's emotion and be rationale in given situations is important and very necessary for every Stoic to know. But this doesn't define a Stoic or Stoicism as a philosophy. The key message of Stoicism is not to build an emotionless machine or to eliminate emotions but to know and learn to live life the best possible way.

In other words, the principle of emotions is like that of virtue in Stoicism; it is important and essential to achieving happiness but it is not the main message of Stoicism, rather living life the right way is the main aim of this ancient philosophy.

The principle of emotions is one of the major aspects of Stoicism. This principle simply revolves around the ability for Stoics to live through life without letting emotions like sadness, anger, pain, and distress affect their way of life or a decision that needs to be taken (rationality or indifference). It is the ability to accept the trials of life without letting them affect your daily routines. In other words, bad things will happen, but that shouldn't hold you back because life will always continue.

Emotions in Stoicism

Emotion in Stoicism goes deeper than the popular notion that Stoics repress or suppress emotion, when in fact, Stoics believe that a well-lived life is an outcome of joy and tranquility. As students and practitioners, Stoics learn and understand how we fit into the universe, which includes all the difficult and strange interactions of life.

Emotions are an affective state of mind where a being experiences hate, joy, sorrow, or fear. Emotions are distinguished from volitional and cognitive states of consciousness.

Despite the fact that a human mind is an impressive tool, Stoics understand that emotions are just part of the mental framework. Emotions are given regard in Stoicism, but are not given full regard, and decisions are based on rationality.

Stoics have a unique approach to the issue of emotions. Take, for instance, if there is hard rain pouring down on a Monday, you don't sit back at home and relax. You grab an umbrella or raincoat and find a way to work. This logic is exactly how emotions work in Stoicism. That is to say Stoics do not let emotions define and guide their behaviors; they just treat it like a rainy day, get an umbrella and move on.

In Stoicism, a person is expected to act well even when experiencing a strong, negative emotion like anger. Stoics believe that a feeling like anger or outburst is irrelevant, as it could have been avoided in the first place because anger itself is a result of taking up an unhealthy perspective which is against Stoic doctrines. Another reason why anger would be an irrelevant option for a Stoic is that they will actually opt for virtue over a bad feeling or emotion, hence avoiding anger.

Stoicism acknowledges three good feelings or emotions in their doctrine called "hai eupatheiai" in the Greek language. These three good feeling were created in contrast to the passion which can also be referred to as "bad feelings."

Below is the list of the three good feelings in contrast with the three bad feelings.

1. Joy versus Pleasure
2. Wish versus Lust/Appetite
3. Caution versus Fear.

The above list is definitely an odd one; but with a lot of background info and research, we should be able to deduce why the ancient Stoics came to these conclusions.

Joy versus Pleasure

Joy according to Stoics is attained by the wise, while pleasure, on the other hand, is considered to be a vice.

In Stoicism, Joy is seen as the elevation of spirit as a result of truth in goodness and truth in possession. For instance, Joy is when one first holds their child in their arms. This scene is considered a joyful one, not because of the immediate feeling you derive from it but the fact that the feeling of joy will never cease and never change to an opposite situation.

Pleasure, on the other hand, is not like the joy that lasts for a long time. It is usually a short satisfaction that can be taken away from you quickly.

In order words, joy is like true happiness that can last a long time, while pleasure is only for a period of time. That is to say, true peace isn't derived from external things, but rather from joy within.

Wish versus Lust/Appetite

To answer the question of why the Stoics consider wishing a good emotion and lust or appetite a bad one, we have to reference back to one of Marcus Aurelius' quotes which goes like this, "Consider the activity it is possible for you to carry out." This quote simply explains that Stoics consider pinning for things you don't have as a bad habit and a waste of time.

Stoics define appetite as a desire or pursuit of an expected situation in an irrational way. (Let's not forget that one of the bases of Stoicism is rationality). For example, enmity is an appetite for revenge and greed is an appetite for material things.

The feeling of appetite is unacceptable in Stoicism as the energy and fantasy derived from this feeling only promote unproductive actions. Don't forget that Stoics don't base their happiness on things that are out of their hands; so it is preferable to wish rather than have an appetite for something.

Why Do Stoics Prefer Wish Over Appetite?

Wish in Stoicism has to do with wanting something, but being contented whether you get it or not. In order words, your contentment is not based on possessing what you want, which is the case in appetite. Wish is a situation of appreciating and wanting the many good things of life -but not letting those many good things become your source of contentment.

Caution versus Fear

Caution versus fear takes the same logic as joy versus pleasure. Fear is an irrational way of avoiding expected danger. Fear suppresses the contentment we feel in the present because we think it will be taken away from us later. Now in Stoicism, this feeling of fear is classified as an irrelevant and unnecessary irrationality.

Caution, on the other hand, has to do with preparation. Stoics believe that with caution, a person should understand that life is filled with ups and down and as a result of this, preparations should be laid down for all the difficulties of life. In order to properly progress in life, we have to approach the world with wariness and awareness.

Emotional Control

Having understood the idea of emotions in Stoicism, the feelings that are accepted and those that are considered wrong, we can safely conclude that a Stoic has the capacity to apply reason to their every action. This is to say, emotions will definitely arise, but these emotions will be subject to rationality and virtue - virtues being wisdom, courage, moderation, and justice.

So basically, in Stoicism, its practitioners are taught to regard desire, passion, and any form of emotion as indifferent.

Here's a quote from Marcus Aurelius' book, *Meditation*, to further explain the concept of emotional control in Stoicism:

"Make sure that the ruling and sovereign part of your soul remains unexpected by every movement, smooth or violent, in your flesh and that it does not combine with them, but circumscribes itself and restricts these experiences to the bodily parts. Whenever they communicate themselves with the mind by virtue of that other sympathy as is bound to occur in a unified organism, you should not attempt to resist the temptation which is a natural one, but you must not allow the ruling center to add its own further judgment that the experience is good or bad." (Meditation 5.26)

This goes to say that Stoics have the ability to feel emotions to the highest degree, but with restrictions. Virtue should always be on stand by to put these emotions in check. In essence, this explanation is what is regarded as emotional control in this ancient philosophy.

Furthermore, Stoicism and actions are considered to work hand in hand. A Stoic is always prepared to act; he does not wait. He acts despite the difficulty and the challenge of the situation at hand. This is because, over time, a Stoic or Sage has been able to practice the power to overcome different emotional barriers.

Finally, what makes a wise man unique and different from a foolish man is his ability to put whatever happens to him to the test of his reasoning and act with a rational response. Emotions, if not controlled, might be the end of us. A lot of hasty decisions and judgments have left a lot of people in deep trouble. Thus, one should be able to separate their emotions from clouding their judgment.

Eliminating emotions is the beginning of reaching greater heights in one's life. Eliminating emotions is the pathway that leads to being logical, which is our next chapter. Immerse yourself in logical reasoning at all times, and watch yourself grow in grace and happiness.

Chapter Seven

Being Logical at All Times

Stoicism over the years has finally been recognized for its many contributions to the philosophy of the mind. One of the key principles of Stoicism that have been linked with the modern day philosophy of the mind is the ability of Stoics to be logical in their thinking at all times.

Logic

Logic in Stoicism is based on preposition logic. This deals with the use of facts and argument flow. The fact here simply has to do with truth and false of a situation. Stoically, preposition logic is referred to as assertables.

Background of Stoic Logic

The Stoics' philosophy of logic was regarded as one of the greatest and most generally accepted philosophies out of two in the classical world. By the 4th century BCE, the Stoic logic philosophy started to originate in a philosophical school called the Megarian school. Diodorus Cronus and his pupil, Philo, developed their own theories of Modality and cognitive prepositions.

Zeno, the father of Stoicism, also studied under the Megarian school and was said to be a fellow pupil like Philo. He applied the philosophy of logic to Stoicism, but it was this philosophy, largely propounded and promoted by the third head of Stoic teachings in the third century BCE , Chryssipus of Soli. Chryssipus' Stoic logic was largely based on the analyzing of situations based on prepositions (true or false).

An integral and important part of the logic in Stoicism is assertability. That goes to say the basic unit of a Stoic logic is an assertable. Assertables are contents of a statement which have a truth value in the sense that, at any time, the statement is true or false. Stoic logic focuses on analyzing choices and consequences, hence creating preposition with connections like "if and then" "either and or" and "nit both." These connections are part of daily reasoning.

Logic is the aspect of Stoicism that examines and analyzes reason. Going further, we can say that for a person to achieve a happy and worthy life, they have to apply logical reasoning with their actions. Stoics also believe that to understand ethics, one has to apply logic to their thoughts and reasoning.

Brand Inwood described the stoics to believe that, "Logic helps a person see the case, reason effectively about practical ideas, stand his or her ground amid confusion, differentiate the certain from the probable, and so forth".

We all have those moments when we say or do something foolish because our emotions made us. You decide to wait for the last minute to finish your work because you'd rather watch Breaking Bad, resulting in a last-minute panic. Or you lean in to kiss a friend because it felt right, only to be pushed away. If nothing else, emotions make life interesting.

But for the most part, we like to think that we're rational decision makers. To make choices, we consider our options and chose the one that makes the most sense. We're not willy-nilly about such things. And those foolish, emotion-based decisions are a rarity, not the norm. As Samuel Johnson once said, "We may take Fancy for our companion, but must follow reason as our guide."

Moreover, most of our public discourse assumes that we are rational. Philosophy, in particular, has tended to focus on logic and reason. The Stoics are one famous example, but Socrates also prided logic over emotion, even to the point of death. Some exceptions exist, like Nietzsche and Rousseau, but they are precisely that - exceptions.

Indeed, most of us like to think that we control our destiny with a rational choice—whether it's in buying a car or choosing a profession—but research shows we may not be as rational as we think.

To understand this fact first requires us to change our view on emotions. Most people see emotions in light of the feelings attached to them—the subjective experience of being happy, sad, or otherwise. When people are sad, they feel sad. It's a subjective mental state, nothing more.

Being logical doesn't mean we should let go of our emotions. As a matter of fact, we can't. No matter how we much feel we can stay away from the tons of emotions we feel every day, we will only end up deceiving ourselves in the long run. However, we can tweak our minds with respect to how we want it to feel.

When we apply logic in our daily life, we ensure things are done in an appropriate manner. Decisions are made only after weighing the consequences, actions are executed only after checking how they will influence the future. Now, that is the right way of doing things. If we end up rushing into something without properly taking a good look at it, we might be jumping into what is not right for us.

Logic is being applied to our daily lives. Talk about economic life, psychological well-being, in relationships, at work, at the shop - in fact, in anything we do. Stoics see logic as the will to reason. Practice Stoicism in your life and watch how you will start placing logic to every of your decision.

Logic is life itself. The great men you adore today applied logic more than a few times in the course of their lives. Thus, if you would wish to emulate them, be sure to hold logic very close to you.

Chapter Eight

Living a Stress-Free Life

In the previous chapters, we discussed how to remain completely happy by following the philosophy of the Stoics. Eliminating sentiments and emotions, staying true to logical reasoning, irrespective of the magnitude and attachment the situation or circumstance may hold, and sticking closely with virtue instead of immorality, is the key to real peace and happiness.

I'm sure you are familiar with the saying "one good turn deserves another," right? And also "what goes around surely comes back around?" Well, that is what Stoicism preaches. Be good to one another, but definitely not emotional to the point of being influenced by your feelings.

All these translate to one thing; living a stress-free life. Stress is both a necessary and unnecessary fatigue which builds up in our bodies due to many reasons we know or we don't even know. Stress can be accumulated in our body via a continuous stressful activity we keep engaging ourselves in. It can also be psychological.

As a matter of fact, stress can take on different forms, in the long run, achieving the same purpose - making you feel down, tired, and unhappy. A lot of surveys and studies have been carried out over the years amongst adults on the levels of self-reported stress and the results came out quite overwhelming and alarming.

Many of them complained of stress from their work due to pressure mounted on them by their superiors or even employers. Some of them complained of the economy as their stress-motivating factor. Others laid their blame on their relationships, thereby feeling stressed in the long run.

Mind you, this book is not to give you a solution on how to bounce back economically. If that is your motive, then you are obviously in the wrong place. However, it will give you an insight on how to lift that pressure and stress off your chest, thereby making you feel free, glowing with joy, and most importantly, become truly happy.

Now, here is a question you should ask yourself. Are you stressed? If I am, what should I do? It is important to know that drinking a whole bottle of champagne won't wash your stress away, nor would swimming in the pool of cannabis wash off the stench of stress from your body. What you can do is quite simple – practice Stoicism.

It the best ticket you can get to take you out of that mess. And guess what? Stoicism is absolutely free. I'm sure you are more familiar with the term now than before, especially after reading through our previous educative and informative chapters. But let's do a quick recap, shall we?

Stoicism is a total way of life - the gateway to achieving complete happiness and tranquility. It encompasses esteemed areas of philosophy like ethics, physics, virtue, nature, and so many more. It focuses on the relationship between man and nature. It is also attributed to living a good and happy life. When you are a Stoic, you make logical decisions and judgments devoid of emotions and sentiments.

Be that as it may, living according to nature guarantees us a stress-free life. When you live life just as the creator had created us to have lived it, you are bound to be completely free from stress of any kind. And that entails being good to our fellow humans and nature in general. That is the only way we can live a stress-free life.

Rationality, zeal to succeed, seeking knowledge, understanding of the cosmos, and so much more are all part of Stoicism. If we behave the way we are truly meant to behave, then we will be extremely and supremely happy. This will, in turn, make living very easy and stress-free.

How to Live a Stress-Free Life Stoically

1.   Control Your Situation: Have you ever wondered why lots of people end up not getting anything right in their lives? Why do they keep failing at everything they have tried working on? Why do they just feel stressed after many trials and end up giving up so easily? It's because they don't have control of the situation. No one has total control of his or her situation more than one who beats an addiction.

Firstly, know the things you have control over. It is important to make this distinction, then differentiate it from what we don't have control over. For instance, if watching porn is what you can not control, irrespective of how hard you try to gain control over it, then it's better we differentiate that from the others.

Knowing these differences between your strength and weaknesses is an added advantage.

2.   Know the Real Problem from Abstract Ones: Imaginary problems and issues have given lots of people more stress than the present ones. I'm sure we are very popular with these words "what if…" We now start getting worried over what is not even a problem to begin with. Then stress starts accumulating in our bodies.

"What is" should really be the concern of our life and not "what might." If we actually start thinking of the present problems in our lives, we will realize that our minds would be focused on finding a solution. But an imaginary problem causes us undeserved and unnecessary stress.

We might be broke tomorrow, but we still have something to hold on to today. We might be homeless tomorrow, but we still have a good house that gives us shelter today. We might be jobless tomorrow, but let's focus on today's job which puts food on our table. Thus, do not start feeling pressured unnecessarily.

3. Know What You Need: Knowing the things you need is vital in living a stress-free life. What are the things you really need? Have you ever taken a moment to think deeply about that question? Don't think in a materialist manner, but as a rational human being.

What are the things you really need to live a happy life? Does keeping a large circle bring you happiness? How about living a materialistic life? Would it make your life less stressful? These and more are the important questions we need to ask ourselves in order to know what we really want.

It is important to know that gaining a stress-free life Stoically is not an easy journey. It means we live our lives while letting go of desires, pleasures, and pains. Forgoing these desires and wants might seem confusing at first, but in the long run, it is for our own good.

4. Cultivate Your Inner Self: All that we are trying to discuss boils down to your inner self. Having total control of your condition and situation is the key to living a stress-free life. You will agree with me that we are not in control of the economy. We are also not in control of what happens in the next five minutes of our lives.

Additionally, we are not in control of our relationships. But one thing we can control is our state of mind and how we make our decisions and judgments. How we relate with other people and nature in general, and our drive towards living a good life will determine if we will end up being happy or not.

A true Stoic believes that a peasant can be most happy if he lives the life of a Sage. On the other hand, a king could live a miserable life unless he ends up living like a Sage. The rules of living are quite different from that of a peasant to a king.

Where a king has many opportunities to lead a good life, a peasant is only limited to few opportunities. In other words, our opportunities for living a good life vary, yet it is only possible for one who has total control of his or her inner self.

A stress-free life is all we all want, no matter the method we decide to follow. Whether we pay a therapist to talk us through it or we practice Stoicism all by ourselves, the end result will still be the same – wanting a stress-free life. With that being said, do not allow depression to take that sanity away from you.

Yes, you saw that right; DEPRESSION! Read on to the next chapter as we open your mind on how to overcome this silent evil.

Chapter Nine

Beating Depression with Stoicism

According to the words of Marcus Aurelius, "Never let the future disturb you. You will meet it, if you have to, with the same weapons of reason which today arm you against the present."

This statement says it all. Why feel depressed when the future is still far? Most times, we forget that we have no control over some things in our lives. Thus, we end up hurting ourselves, feeling really depressed, and shutting everyone out of our lives.

Depression, according to a concise English dictionary is the mental state characterized by a pessimistic sense of inadequacy and despondent lack of activity. In other words, it is a sunken stage in a person's life which is characterized by sad feelings of gloom and inadequacies. If you happen to find yourself or a friend curling up alone in the confines of a bed, looking dejected and hopeless, then you or that particular person is depressed.

Depression eats deep and is present in a person for a long time before it manifests. The pain one feels is directed inward, with lots of negative thoughts running through the mind. Life will feel meaningless, if not a waste of space.

One would start withdrawing into their shells and comfort zones. Your life would seem like an embarrassment, even to you. And there would be no better way of ending it all than to take one's life. In as much as depression is real and present in today's world, it is not true to say that depression cannot be curbed and managed.

It is a passing phase in one's life which could be passed successfully with the right means or methods. Talking and reaching out to friends helps, getting a new passion or hobby helps, and meeting new people is also great. But one method that works fast and adequately is following the philosophy and tenets of Stoicism.

We often complain about how life has been unfair, but forget to check ourselves on how to live life in the best possible manner. Stoicism presents us with the perfect alternative for a better life. Now the question remains, are we making good use of this alternative? Are we even trying to live a good life?

Depression comes after we had made a grave mistake in the course of our lives; after we have failed to make great decisions and judgments concerning our lives. That is when depression will begin to set in. It's not the relationship we hold dear that hates us. It is how we relate to these several phenomena that depict our lives.

Stoicism teaches us to be logical in all areas of our lives. It puts logic ahead of sentiments and emotions. It also places virtue high before immorality. Following this way of life will definitely keep depression far away from you. This is why we often imagine why our lives seem to be regressing instead of making progress.

We often picture ourselves at a very high point many years from now and end up moving a little, or not moving at all, toward that point. This is characterized by our way of making decisions and judgments. Change that today and watch yourself grow.

Always be filled with positivity. Negative thoughts or pessimism have a way of pulling us back no matter the amount of hard work we put in. Positivity brings the whole world to our feet. It makes us see anything as achievable no matter the obstacles around it.

Therefore, curbing depression with Stoicism comes with two important questions that must be answered in order to achieve good results. First, we need to ask ourselves where those silly emotions we often feel each time depression wants to set in come from. According to a study conducted by a popular Austrian Neurologist, Sigmund Freud, divided psyche into three parts and he named these parts; ID, EGO, and SUPEREGO.

The ID is the part that holds the instinctive, aggressive, and jealous kinds of emotions. The ID also creates anxiety, especially if the ID is threatened. For instance, ID emotions occur when an over-pampered child gets angry, or even sad. The emotions rage powerfully and quite short.

SUPER-EGO emotions are criticizing oneself. It comes as a result of comparing yourself with another. It also comes with self-loathing, self-criticism, and trying to make yourself into a perfectionist, while EGO is the emotion that erupts while trying to create a balance between both emotions. This is the enemy of man. It is the combination of emotions that might end up overpowering you in the long run.

Stoicism is the realistic solution toward these surges of emotion. It is the only clean, clear method you can use in curbing depression and living a happy life. It builds up your mind to be indifferent to pain and pleasure. It gives you peace of mind, something prayers, hopes, and the words "don't worry," would never give you. Go through the writings of Marcus Aurelius, Epictetus, Seneca, and many other Stoic philosophers.

Immerse yourself to their teachings and life lessons. Your life will definitely take shape - a very nice shape. Stoicism would give you a pathway toward accepting nature. It prepares your mind for the worst. Life can be quite tough. Thus, Stoicism will prepare your mind to stay clear-headed and maintain complete focus in reaching your set out goals.

In the words of Nassim Nicholas Taleb, "A Stoic is someone who transforms fear into prudence, pain into transformation, mistakes into initiation, and desires into undertaking."

That way, one would maintain indifference to the pains and hardships of life, thereby remaining focus and clear-headed. In other words, our path would be set right before us, and our mistakes would be perceived and corrected. Stoicism helps us point out which part of our decisions are clearly irrational. It serves as a guiding principle toward making better judgments. It preaches to us about taking a second look at our decisions and judgments before executing them.

How to overcome depression

1. Inner Control: According to the words of Epictetus, we should "Remember, it is not enough to be hit or insulted to be harmed, you must believe that you are being harmed. If someone succeeds in provoking you, realize your mind is complicit in the provocation. Which is why it is essential that we do not respond impulsively to impressions; take a moment before reacting, and you will find it easier to maintain control."

No Stoic principle beats having inner control of oneself. It is important to know that one's thoughts are exactly what one needs to master before gaining control of the total body. For example, you can train your mind to start thinking positively and seeing life from a whole new angle. Thus, the kind of thoughts your mind would produce would be definitely toward the way you had configured it.

Controlling oneself can be quite difficult, especially when one has an addiction. However, even after configuring our thinking style, we might still find it very difficult to resist being influenced by our emotions. Therefore, practicing Stoicism continuously is the key to having total control of the mind, which will in turn help in creating a stress free life for us all.

2. Personal Responsibility: As Marcus Aurelius rightly puts it, "And see that you keep a cheerful demeanor and retain your independence of outside help and the peace which others can give. Your duty is to stand straight – not held straight."

Many times, we have done things that we aren't even proud of, thus, looking the other way. Many times we have neglected our sense of responsibility not because we don't want to but because we are ashamed to. This is against Stoicism. We all are accountable to our deeds and actions.

We need to take charge of our lives if really we want to live a happy and stress-free life. Challenge yourself to making the right decisions, so as not to be burdened with taking responsibility for what you aren't proud of. You are your own master. Instead of being the normal complainer, Stoicism will teach you to be an actual rational thinker as you face your problems.

The feeling that comes with taking responsibility is quite amazing.

3. The Future/Success: Dreaming about a beautiful and amazing future just won't do the trick for you. Don't get me wrong, dreaming is quite good. As a matter of fact, it is the first thing great men do before achieving their insurmountable feats. So dream of the future with big success, but are you ready to make that dream a reality?

No matter the outcome of your dream, whether good or bad, sitting down and doing nothing or even giving up after the first try is not the right way to go about it. Remember, Stoics do not give up. Keep striving hard, keep pushing, keep working, until you see the light. What Stoicism will do is configure your mind positively, so as to be strong and not be influenced with your emotions, because trust me, fear would come.

To this effect, allow me to end this with the golden words of Marcus Aurelius. "Have the acts of a man with an eye for precisely what needs to be done, not in the glory of its doing."

4.　Death: Seneca once said, "Death: there's nothing bad about it at all except the thing that comes before it – the fear of it."

Death shouldn't be a thing of fear for us, but instead something that should boost our morale and hope in living a better life. Many of us get scared the moment death is being mentioned. Little wonder why people gather more in a celebration than in a funeral. But, like it or not, death is inevitable.

But the real question you should ask yourself is, what then should we do with our life before death comes knocking on our door? Are we going to keep being depressed or dust of our behind and start taking charge of our lives? Stoicism will help you focus on life itself; how best to utilize every breath you take in and out. How you can make your life meaningful to you and nature

Depression is real in case many of you don't believe so. Have you ever been in a state where everything starts going from bad to worse? Nothing hurts more than that feeling. You start feeling like a loser, like your life is a total joke. Be that as it may, Stoicism will help you beat it and give you the real happiness you truly deserve.

Chapter Ten

Being Calm Amidst Adversities

What many of us lack is the ability to remain calm and collected even in the face of adversities, tribulations, and obstacles. Great men don't fidget, no matter the circumstances. They remain focused and geared toward doing something great or achieving a massive feat for themselves. That is one secret they will never tell you.

Only a few would like to share the secret to their success and happy life. Zeno of Citium faced lots of criticism in the course of propagating his philosophy. Apple's big man, Steve Jobs also faced his own tribulations before becoming the co-founder of one of the world 's leading gadget-producing company.

This same process goes for all other great men before climbing to the position of authority and power. As a child, Aliko Dangote, the most successful black man alive, sold sweets in school as a young boy. He remained calm and in control of his life before things turned to his favor years later.

Being a stoic comes with its own share of problems. Life is not going to be nice because you made a resolution to be good and live by virtue. But, don't let it weigh you down; instead remain calm. This is one of the qualities of a true Stoic; the ability to remain calm and still maintain the relationship between yourself and nature, even when things go south.

Life often comes up with events that may seem to be over us. The more we solve these problems, the more other ones keep springing up. Stoicism will help you establish stability and control over your life. Why create problems for ourselves when we can actually avoid them completely if we practice Stoicism?

To be fair, most of these problems we find ourselves with are creations of our own doing. If only we could keep records of our daily lives and activities, we would be able to pinpoint the errors and mistakes we make every single day. Thus, Stoicism keeps your focus instead of derailing from your goal. It charges you up until you feel calm, in control, and secure.

Even in the face of tribulations, learn to separate your emotions, feelings, passion, and desires. This will give you a clear head to sail through the raging tides of adversities right before you. Stoicism principles teach us that life still continues even in the face of adversities. These principles should govern your mind as a Stoic, so that if failure looms, adaptation becomes necessary.

The ultimate goal of Stoicism is to give inner peace to man. Achieving this inner peace comes from dealing with problems calmly and maturely. However, in order to scale through a problem, we must understand that problem first. We must be able to transform our problems into the fuel that feeds our fires.

Epictetus rose from a slave to a philosopher. However, this didn't come easy. He had to master his present condition before transforming it into his blessing. The same goes for Marcus Aurelius. He faced lots of tribulations like any Stoic you will find. Yet, he stayed calm amidst those adversities. Seneca was also a statesman who had written lots of letters and essays on the importance of staying calm amidst adversities.

Do you want to live life like this great Stoic thinkers? Then immerse yourself to these three philosophies:

1. Accept That Emotions Come From Within: Marcus Aurelius wrote, "Today I escaped anxiety. Or no, I discarded it, because it was within me, in my own perceptions – not outside."

It is important to know that outside forces can not influence or make us feel bad. The emotions we feel come from within (inside us). It is very easy to lay blame on the outside world and phenomena, but the truth remains, all conflicts begin from within.

When we run away from our problems, from reality, we tend to prolong these problems in our lives, thereby harming ourselves even more. Thus, the next time you find yourself deep in a problem, don't look at the outside for solution, but look inward. Thus, instead of running away from your problems, face them instead.

2. Get a Mentor That Teaches You Honesty: One of the greatest virtues is honesty. Honesty in words and deeds can take you out of nowhere to somewhere. According to the words of Seneca, "Choose someone whose way of life as well as words, and whose very face as mirroring the character that lies behind it, have won your approval. Be always pointing him out to yourself either as your guardian or as your model. This is a need, in my view, for someone as a standard against which our character can measure themselves. Without a ruler to do it against you won't make it crooked straight."

Check yourself first before choosing who to be your mentor. You and your mentor must have something in common – same goals, same beliefs, or same ideology. That way, you can be sure to blend in with the ways of your guardian. For example, as a writer, you might want to get someone that would guide you on your path to being formidable in the field of writing.

You might want someone to brush your crude skills and pull you through until you come out better. Irrespective of your profession, situation, and circumstance, there is always someone you can learn a thing or two from. Immerse yourself within their life; learn lessons from their stories and works, their successes and failures, their strengths and weaknesses, and so much more.

One important thing to know is that this is not a competition nor a comparison. As a matter of fact, it isn't about using the life of your mentor as a benchmark or yardstick for reaching your goals. Also, even after emulating our mentor, our lives might not be exactly what we want or success might not come immediately. Therefore, stay calm and be patient. Everyone has someone they can look up to.

3. Acknowledge Life after Failure: The failure of a man is not the end of his life. Even after failing, one must pick himself back up and forge ahead continuously. Abraham Lincoln, who became the president of the United States in 1960, also had his fair share of failures which he didn't let deter him from reaching his goal.

He lost more than he won and still, he is celebrated to date. According to the words of Marcus Aurelius, "Does what happened to keep you from acting with justice, generosity, self-control, sanity, prudence, honesty, humility, straightforwardness, and all other qualities that allow a person's nature to fulfill itself? So remember this principle when something threatens to cause you pain: the thing itself is no misfortune at all; to endure it and prevail is great good fortune."

People won't always give you a pat on the back for every idea that comes out of your head. Most times, they will even criticize you and tag you a failure. That shouldn't get to you. Instead, transform this failure into something great in order to come out even better and stronger.

How to Remain Calm with Stoicism

1. **Live in the Present:** Have you ever thought about the future? What life holds for you in the next five to ten years of your life? These and many more questions are what puts fear and anxiety into us, thereby making us lose focus on the present. We forget that our present makes the future.

Most times, we are mostly carried away by the glitters and glamour of life. We tend to get carried away by what life offers. For example, the rise of technology has brought the likes of sophisticated gadgets and devices which can be very distracting. Let's cultivate the habit of being in the present and make the best out of what we have and where we find ourselves.

2. **Be Thankful:** Always be thankful to people around you, no matter the circumstances. It is the little gratitude you give that will lead to higher altitudes. Most times, we tend to not give actual thanks to the people behind our smiles and successes, especially if things start going our way. We will now start thinking it's our effort and hard work that got us where we are.

   That might be true. But one thing that is also true is that you alone didn't achieve the feat. Be thankful even to the smallest person that helped you climb the ladder to success. Saying thank you doesn't even cost a thing. But the effect it holds on people is quite scintillating.

   Be thankful for everything you've got. Be thankful for who ever stood by you through trying times or difficult moments. Be thankful for the food you eat. Be thankful for your family standing by you. There are more than a thousand things we should be thankful for every day of our lives. Cultivate the habit of being thankful and watch yourself grow.

3. **Eliminate Attachments:** Attachments, emotions, feelings, sentiments, and so on are all the same thing, no matter how much you try to twist the name. In the lives of the majority, these terms rule their world completely. Little wonder why they don't get to make good decisions and judgements, thereby causing them to make mistakes that may cause them something grave in the long run.

Stoicism preaches their elimination from our lives. A total elimination of these terms in our lives will find us calm, even in the face of adversities. We will be able to face any tribulations or obstacles standing in our way, without fidgeting.

4. **Hold Time Dear:** Time is everything, but time waits for no one. Technology and science have been able to invent sophisticated and scintillating machines, ideas, and so much more. But one of the things they haven't been able to invent is the machine to stop time. Thus, my friend, hold time dear. However, we are not saying you start hurrying through life. We are also not saying you start jumping some steps, cutting corners, and even duplicating phases just to reach your goal faster and illegitimately. That wouldn't be right and cool.

   Instead, always ensure you are doing the right thing at the right time. Efficiency and effectiveness should be your right hand men. Always have it at the back of your mind that death can come for us at any time. Thus, use it as a guiding factor toward reaching your goals.

5. **Stop Procrastinating; Do it Now:** Procrastination has a way of making us lazy and useless in the long run. Imagine shifting an hour work for as long as ever knowing fully well that it is vital to our survival. Crazy right? When we start saying "I'll do it later," we are creating room for a beast of laziness in us.

   We won't realize that until we start seeing the damage delay had done to us. Ensure you cultivate the habit of doing it now. That is when your life will take shape. If we start doing everything at the exact time we ought to have done it, our life will definitely become far better than the way it is. Procrastination will definitely hold you back from achieving this.

6. **Prioritize:** Even in Economics, there is room for making your topmost priority list. This is called a Scale of Preference. Take your time and make your scale of preference. Start from the least important things in your life and end with the most important things you hold dear.

    Notwithstanding, we don't have to get rid of anything before we make our priorities right. The reason why we've not been making that progress we had envisioned is because of our misplaced priorities. Instead of letting go of what drags us behind, let's try and look for a whole new angle.

    What exactly can we do to make those things become useful to us? For example, social media can be quite crazy. The glamour, the limelight, the attention, and so much more, can be quite intriguing and deceiving. Even if it may slow your progress, you can't say you'd want to throw it away all of a sudden. Instead, tweak your activities on it to make your life more colorful.

7. **Be Honest:** Honesty in words and deeds is a trait that can be very hard to come by in this modern world we live in. People hardly tell the truth these days. They believe being honest will do nothing but get you killed. That might be true. But isn't it better to die honorably than to live as a pathetic liar?

    Try and see through yourself and check that you are clean before you start laying criticism on others around you. Be a good example to others by following the path of honesty and righteousness. That is the only way you will be calm even in the face of adversities. When your hands are clean, you'll have nothing to worry about.

Follow these guidelines and watch how calmness will reign over you completely, even in the face of adversity. Train your mind, don't cut corners, and accept everything as the will of God. That is the only way you can truly be happy. The next chapter will include the true meaning of indifference. Read through as we clear all misconceptions and misrepresentations of the word "INDIFFERENCE."

Chapter Eleven

Indifference: Unveiling the Goodness in You

The word Stoicism has been considered synonymous with indifference more often not. Each time we hear the word Stoicism, indifference comes to mind. But the question we should ask ourselves is, "Indifference to what?" Most times, emotions are very hard to let go of. They come as a result of the way we absorb events and happenings around us.

A typical businessman would feel very bad at the sight of a loss, thereby losing focus on the business. This would be evident in the kinds of decisions he made henceforth. Indifference in Stoicism is a very large concept and equally provocative. A lot of people characterized it, with Stoics, to mean indifference to anything and everything.

Indifference to pleasure, indifference to pain, indifference to wealth, indifference to our emotions, and so much more. They now begin to think Stoics don't really care about anything at all. This is very wrong. It's the misconception and the misrepresentation of the concept propagated mostly by the modern Stoics.

Be that as it may, true Stoics aren't indifferent in that manner at all. What indifference means to Stoics is that they believe and trust in the order of nature. This belief should be more than enough for one to stop feeling drawn toward expectations and desires.

A strong belief in fate strengthens one's indifferent stand. When you are indifferent, you don't need anything to go a certain and actual way. You just lay back, take a deep breath, and watch nature work its magic.

This is one perfect way of being stress-free, staying away from depression, and being genuinely happy. Stoicism gives you that push you need toward loving yourself. Indifference gives you the strength to push further without wanting the irrelevant freebies and bonuses. It builds your mind up to scaling through even greater obstacles in your life.

Indifference to the pain and pleasure of life comes as a result of configuring one's mind toward the path of eudemonia. Accept both good and evil as they come, knowing full-well that we can only do little or nothing to change it. As Marcus Aurelius rightly puts it, "Whatever happens to you has been waiting to happen since the beginning of time. The twining strands of fate wove both of them together: your own existence and the things that happen to you."

As an important concept of Stoicism, indifference comes with being calm and resilient toward our problems, the ability to pass through that phase without feeling any kind of emotion. Daniel, who is a janitor at a prestigious telecommunication firm, comes in smiling and goes out with no worries at all.

Many will always wonder what his secret was. Daniel doesn't even make up to six figures a year. He is also clearly not living the American dream, but he exudes so much love and happiness. Well, it's pretty simple! Daniel has found a new path to living a happy life. He has embraced Stoicism, thereby becoming indifferent to the events, happenings, and circumstances revolving around him.

Be that as it may, only a true and patient Stoic can attain complete indifference. This is the only way to achieve complete peace and serenity. According to Stoicism, it is not what you endure that matters, but how you endure it. Indifference is not only about accepting what life throws at us. It is about how well we handle and take care of the problems.

Thus, giving up is not an option with Stoics. Being depressed is also not an option. Let take an example from the life and lessons of Seneca, one of Stoicism's powerhouses. His friend, Lucilius, had sought his advice on more than one occasion. This particular experience was remarkable.

Lucilius, as a civil servant, had a lawsuit against him which would soil his reputation down the mud, thereby putting an end to his political career. Seneca writes him a letter, telling Lucilius to place himself in the worst possible situation, thereby preparing his mind for the worst possible outcome.

This helped Lucilius in seeing the situation from a whole new perspective, thereby becoming indifferent and accepting any possible outcome in clean faith. Indifference should be the cornerstone of all Stoic beliefs. Lucilius realized that Seneca was providing him with a path toward inner peace, reconciliation, and being comfortable even the midst of tribulations.

Others would have gone into depression - or even contemplated suicide in general. But instead, Seneca told his friend to consider the act of Stoicism. Seneca made an example of himself. He had also witnessed a great slump – an exile, ridicule, humiliation, and bankruptcy. Yet, he remained string, configured his mind into being indifferent, and came back even stronger.

The tribulations and struggles of our lives shouldn't be the end of everything for us. Instead, it should be the fuel that feeds our fire of survival. It should be the gateway toward the start of a new beginning. A stoic should always hope for the best while expecting the worst in any situation.

Be that as it may, go out there; embrace your life and all events that unfold afterward with open arms. Feeling bad about anything won't change the outcome of the situation. Instead, make the best of it.

Just like the saying goes, "When life throws you a lemon, you make lemonade."

Listen, we do not have control over everything that has happened or is even what is happening to us right now. Sometimes, we might not even know how these things happen. So, do not worry or even get sad about it. Instead, be sure to make the best out of the situation. Remember, there is nothing like giving up in the Stoics' dictionary. No matter how much you keep falling, learn to pick yourself back up every time.

Our level of tenacity and perseverance differs from each other. Thus, the rate at which we generally recoup from a loss, downfall, or even a disaster also differs. To this effect, what might work for you might not work for me. Try different Stoicism techniques as much as you want until you master your preferred techniques.

You might decide to meditate, retrace your steps back, and think about the previous decisions and judgements you've made. Walk through the park to clear your head, if possible. Do you have a car? Even better. Drive around and around until your start feeling yourself again. This would only mean one thing, trying to feel unperturbed.

The state of being unperturbed can also be known as ataraxia. It is the complete phase in our lives where we gain total freedom from worry, distress, and anger. In other words, it is known as having a peace of mind and being totally subdued by calmness and serenity. Reaching the state of atatraxia is the ultimate goal of every Stoic.

Nevertheless, pleasure is not something to flee from, at least not for Stoics. It is an important part of our life we must learn to understand and control. Only when we hold total control of it do we would know how and when to apply it in our daily lives. Additionally, pleasure can only be applied successfully and correctly if it is applied in line with virtue.

Virtue is the light that shines on the path of Stoicism. Pleasure without its guiding principle, virtue, would leave you reckless and irrational, thus making your life irresponsible. No one prays not to have or experience the pleasures of life. Life can be quite boring without pleasure, except if you are a monk.

Stoicism will show you the world in a whole new angle; that is being indifferent. You will definitely experience pain and pleasure, but how you react and control these emotions is what matters. Cultivate a strong mind and train yourself well in controlling your emotions toward pleasure or pain.

Failure to train yourself can lead to your downfall, or even ruin. However, a perfectly trained mind would be able to differentiate both pains and pleasures from influencing our emotions, thereby maintaining an indifferent stand when these emotions sprout out.

Just as what you hold dear today can be used against you, anything you once cherished can also be used against you if you don't play your cards right. Therefore, the only way to be on a safer side is not to even feel attached to anything in general. That way, it would be hard to have a weakness.

Thus, according to Seneca, enjoying the pleasures that come from our hard work or even good fortune is not a bad thing. However, we should always put it at the back of our mind that those things might turn against us someday. Also, we should develop a mind which would enable us to part with it anytime that happens.

With that being said, the key to living a Stoic life is indifference. Indifference unlocks the goodness in you. It opens up your eyes to what you are actually missing after making irrational decisions and judgments. Sometimes, we wish we paid a little more attention to being indifferent to the pains and pleasures of our lives. Indifference puts a stop to depression even before it manifests.

This brings us to our next chapter; practicalizing Stoicism in our daily lives. Trust me, the chapter is awesome and soul-captivating.

Chapter Twelve

A Pinch of Stoicism in Our Daily Lives

A pinch of Stoicism in our lives won't be a bad idea as we strive through the struggles of life. A pinch of goodness and indifference will surely help us maintain a happy and healthy lifestyle.

Like we pointed out in the previous chapters, knowing about Stoicism is not enough. How about studying it? What is the essence of knowing about something without practicing it in our daily lives? Thus, knowing and applying it are two different things entirely. It is the only way we can gain from Stoicism.

In today's world, many of us live our lives recklessly, with no purpose, passion, or drive. Some of us even end up getting depressed after making unwise decision. We keep trying the same methods and techniques that have failed us consistently. Aren't you tired of repeating the same thing over and over again?

Aren't you tired of getting the same heartbreaking results from the irrational decisions and judgments you make? Just a pinch of Stoicism would make a difference. Just a pinch of Stoicism will change your life miraculously. It will equip you with rationality and virtuousness. Here are some of the daily Stoic practices you can actually apply as you go about your daily life.

1. Always Avoid Stress: Marcus Aurelius writes, in *Meditations*, "You have power over your mind — not outside events. Realize this, and you will find strength."

Avoid anything that seems stressful or might cause you stress. Marcus Aurelius is telling us to always look inward for a solution to our problems. We all have the power to control our minds and thoughts one way or the other. Configure your mind in an amazing manner and seek the power to scale through any problem from within yourself. Do not forget to meditate if you have to.

How to Apply: While meditating, jot down your inner thoughts. This will help you remember everything after you are done meditating. Make sure you write out what you can control and what you cannot. The moment you do this, you'll have power over how you react that which you do not control. Trust me there is power in telling the difference between these two.

2. Always Learn to Control Your Anger: As Seneca puts it, "If a man is angry, let us give him time to come to realize what he has done: he will be his own critic."

One of the crazy feelings that had caused more harm than good is our anger. Sometimes, we end up doing dumb stuff just because our anger has taken over us completely. We now start seeing things differently and behaving violently. Seneca was of the opinion that an angry man will definitely see things clearly after he had calmed down.

How to apply: Meditation is the key to anger. Instead of lashing out, breaking things we bought with our money, and doing crazy things to anyone around us, how about you try solitude? When you are angry, always learn to talk less and keep to yourself more. Meditation will make us reach our inner self and give us the calmness we deserve. You can also take a walk or drive around to clear your head. It works.

3. Dealing with Difficult People: No matter how hard we try to avoid people, especially the ones that make our lives difficult, we just can't. They might be our bosses, our colleagues, our relatives, or even our friends. One would get to realize that we are stuck with these people and getting rid of them is not an option. But instead, we learn to get along with them.

Marcus Aurelius said, "Begin each day by telling yourself: Today I shall be meeting with interference, ingratitude, insolence, disloyalty, ill-will, and selfishness — all of them due to the offenders' ignorance of what is good or evil."

How to Apply: One thing we should take note of is that we cannot constantly influence people's decisions and opinions no matter how hard we try. Even if we are able to do that a few times, we won't be able to do that continuously. How about learning to cope with it? Be true and honest to yourself. Never compromise your values and everything will be fine.

When they see that, irrespective of how hard they try, you still remain yourself – humble, loyal, and honest, they will also learn to cope with you. However, continue to be yourself and on your best behavior. That is the only way to deal with difficult people.

4.   **Our Tribulations Can be Utilized:** Ryan Holiday also said that, "The obstacle in the path becomes the path. Never forget, within every obstacle is an opportunity to improve our condition."

Our problems should be the stepping stones towards greatness. If great men of today backed out at the slightest challenge, the world wouldn't be what it is today. Believe it or not, challenges will come. They will come, especially when we least expect them. But, be sure to be ready at all times.

How to Apply: Imagine you are on the verge of getting a multi-million dollar contract with a telecommunication company, but faced a little challenge of facing bankruptcy at that same time. This scenario is a very tense and a crazy moment that will take the Stoic in us to pull through it. Now, would you allow the multi-million dollar contract that will enable you to keep your company from drowning disappear from your grasp or would do all it takes to win?

Stir obstacles in the right direction and they will end up working for you. Make use of your experience and knowledge on how you tackle everyday problems.

5.   Fail Sometimes: Marcus said that, "Does what's happened to keep you from acting with justice, generosity, self-control, sanity, prudence, honesty, humility, straightforwardness, and all other qualities that allow a person's nature to fulfill itself?"

There is no harm in falling down sometimes. We definitely can't win all the time. Thus, when something wants to start causing us pain because we'd fail, always remember this side of Stoicism.

What matters is that we stand up and get walking again. We recalculate our moves and steps, then come back stronger. It is important to know that there is always at least an atom of lesson in our failures. Don't feel pressured. Sometimes, the smell of too much victory and success can be quite intoxicating, thereby getting to our head. Fail sometimes; it will remind you of how hard is it to succeed.

How to Apply: Failure can be overwhelming most times, especially if you are not used to failing. You will now start feeling surprised and angry over your failure. Don't be carried away. Always learn to focus on the bigger picture. Don't feel saddened with everyone looking at you like a loser.

Gather strength from their criticism, learn deep lessons, and know your mistakes. It's the result that matters, trust me. No one cares how many times you've failed. Be the winner everyone wants to associate with. Abraham Lincoln failed more than he won. Today, no one is celebrating him for those failures, but for his tenacity and perseverance to succeed.

Well, that and more are what it entails to live like a Stoic. Like we pointed out before, to know is to forget, to practice is to remember, and practice they say makes perfect. If we keep practicing, we are sure to reach the stage of eudemonia – real happiness according to Stoics. This brings us to our next chapter, how Stoicism opens up a pathway for real happiness, joy, and positivity.

Chapter Thirteen

Stoicism: A Pathway to Joy, Happiness, and Positivity

Happiness is the final outcome of Stoicism. It is why Zeno of Citium coined the philosophy in the first place. How can man truly be happy? What can man do to live a happy life? How does man influence nature into becoming truly happy? No matter how much you try to twist these questions, they will still bring us to one conclusion – Happiness.

We should know that obtaining happiness is not restricted to just one means. There are lots of means one can follow to attain real happiness, even if it may look weird in the beginning. For example, Negative Visualization is one effective way of experiencing happiness. As a matter of fact, early Stoics like Seneca, Epictetus, and Marcus Aurelius had used negative visualization to give themselves hope and happiness even in the face of severe obstacles.

What does Negative Visualization do? How does one visualize negatively in order to achieve long-deserved happiness? It's pretty simple. All we need to do it to configure our mind into picturing the bad side to everything revolving around us. What if things go south? What if it just doesn't go the way we had planned it?

This will certainly make you feel better in the long run and prepared for the worst. It will make you realize how lucky you have been with all the good things surrounding you, thereby encouraging you to count your blessings.

There is no better way of being grateful for the things you have than thinking along negative visualization. These thoughts will, therefore, trigger a grateful emotion in you which will, in turn, put a smile on your face. For example, when we think about all the homeless children which are a result of war, hunger, and destruction going on in their places, we tend to look up and thank God even for the little we have.

To that effect, we are bound to start thanking God for the good life we are enjoying, the peace we have in our environment, and the plenty and plush that surround us. This will, in turn, make us genuinely happy.

It is important to know that no matter how crazy or damaged you might appear to be, negative visualization will definitely give you a sense of gratitude. There is always someone out there who is poorer than you. There is always someone out there who is uglier than you. There is always someone out there who lacks the thing you have and whom you are far better than. So long as you are not dead, there is always a reason to be thankful and grateful.

Like we discussed earlier, negative visualization is the cover that makes you see the world from a whole new angle entirely. Even when we exaggerate our position in life in order to make us feel better, it actually supports it and helps us get exactly what we want – genuine happiness and peace of mind.

Additionally, Stoics are of the view that we can never find the real happiness that we deserve if we don't let go of expectations and hope. If we keep holding on to these two, there will surely be a problem. There is no way we will get a better and clearer picture of our future if we don't detach ourselves from these things.

Happiness should be seen as a present thing. It is not a future prospect. If we are focused on the future while neglecting today, there is no way we will be happy today. This can make us feel depressed and gloomy. At this point, nothing will make sense at all.

The Stoic remedy for this is reflected by the Ralph Ellison quote, "Life is to be lived, not controlled…"

If we keep that in mind, irrespective of how hard reality tries to control or influence our judgments and deductions, we will still remain indifferent and not attached, and we are sure to live a happy life. Additionally, if we stick to the plan of just controlling what is within our power and neglecting but knowing that which we cannot control, then that is the only way we can turn a blind eye to different tons of effect life will throw at us. There is dignity in accepting things as they come.

According to Seneca, "No insane person can be happy, and no one can be sane if he regards what is injurious as the highest good and strives to obtain it. The happy man, therefore, is he who can make the right judgment in all things."

The above quote from Seneca points to the importance of rationality and the elimination of emotions when making judgments. Making a judgment with a disturbed mind would not likely be the best decision when we start reviewing after becoming sober. When the mind is filled with raging emotions, it makes bad decisions along that line.

Imagine making a decision or executing an action right after you just lost your job. The first thing that comes to your mind definitely won't be something positive, as you will go completely blank and your mind far away from reality. It will take the grace of God for one not to do anything stupid. That is the power irrationality holds over us when our mind is clouded.

However, a Stoic will maintain an indifferent stand irrespective of the magnitude of the situation. Not because they don't care. Not because they don't feel pains or pleasures. But because their minds have been trained stoically to be indifferent to any feeling whatsoever. That is the attribute of a true Stoic.

Upholding virtue ahead of immorality also helps in attaining happiness. Been good and exuding virtues are key attributes of a Stoic. Do you really want to be happy? How about you start with this? This is the same thing that had worked for the likes of Marcus Aurelius, Seneca, and Epictetus.

When talking about the importance of virtue, Seneca argues, "What! Does virtue alone suffice to make you happy? Why? Of course, consummate and God-like virtue such as this not only suffices but more than suffices: for when a man is placed beyond the reach of any desire, what can he possibly lack? If all that he needs is concentered in himself, how can he require anything from without? It is that some are tied more or less tightly by these bonds, and some have even tied themselves with them as well; whereas he who has made progress towards the upper regions and raised himself upwards drags a looser chain, and though not yet free, is yet as good as free."

Virtue is everything. Virtue comes with good luck. However, there might be a time when one doesn't even tread the path of virtue and everything will still work in his or her favor. Technically, it might be attributed to mere luck and fortune that follows that person. Which is true. But, one who follows virtue is sure to reap goodness and happiness.

This long quote should tell you the importance of virtue as a principle of Stoicism. With that being said, how about you start wearing your best smile, answering rude or aggressive gestures with a warm smile or calm nod, and being good to all including yourself? That is the only way you can be truly happy and reach the stage of eudemonia.

As we are reaching the ending of this book, we would like to ask if it is becoming boring or getting more interesting? Well, you haven't seen anything yet as we would discuss even more on knowing what to control, what not to control, and how to know the difference in our next chapter.

Chapter Fourteen

After the Storm, Comes Peace

Now that you've learned all that is there to know about Stoicism, we are sure that your mind must understand the principles and tenets. Applying it to achieve peace and genuine happiness is the only step left for you to take. Most times, life presents us with more than what we can truly handle. Instead of giving up, we should learn to cultivate the habit of fighting through it, no matter the circumstances.

Having an in-depth knowledge about Stoicism paves the way for a clearer mind. As a matter of fact, true peace comes when we accept our pain. When we use our pain to forge ahead and create a new path for ourselves, that is true Stoicism.

No one likes pain. In fact, we all try to avoid passing through this phase, by all means necessary, even if it means cutting corners. But, pain is part of our life. It can strengthen our journey and give us a whole meaning to life. It can bring you closer to reality. Pain brings focus and in the long run reveals our true self. However, how to deal with our pain determines how we are turning out to be after the phase ends. Are you going to let your pain beat you up, or stay strong until it subsides?

Stoicism paves the way for us to realize how perfect and great being good will suit us, if only we will try. It shows us the easiest and cheapest path toward living a happy life, especially in line with virtue, rationality, and a perfectly maintained mental state. No one is truly living unless he or she holds nature high and conforms to its laws. Live your life in this manner and watch yourself grow.

The storm isn't over until you've learned to master and know yourself better. Marcus Aurelius didn't become famous for just sitting idle and ordering guards around. He was tactful, intelligent, and ready to see the brighter side of things no matter how sour they got.

To begin with, learn to successfully tweak and configure the way you think in an appropriate manner that will benefit you in the long run. Even Epictetus succumbs to this as he gives the two mitigating principles that guide how we end up or should actually control the things around us.

He agreed that we can control some things that happen around us. We can actually influence them into coming out in our favor. While, on the other hand, some are just completely out of our reach. They are controlled by nature and will end up influencing our lives. Thus, we end up getting unhappy by thinking too much of what we can't control. We even go extra length, thereby creating unnecessary stress for ourselves.

Epictetus continued with his argument by laying emphasis on what we cannot control. As a matter of fact, what we control is very little in comparison to what we can't seem to control. For example, we certainly can control nature. We also can't control how nature would pin its web around us. We can't control people's feelings about us. We can't force them to like us or hate us. Thus, what we can control is ourselves, and our thoughts, which influence our judgments and decisions.

Little wonder why we get mad if things don't go our way, especially we've put in lots of effort. But as the true Stoic we hope to become, shit happens. We now begin to see things around us as a combination of disappointment. Like they aren't working in our favor no matter how hard we try. These are nothing but just figments of our own imagination. They are things we create so as to give ourselves a much-needed excuse when things go south.

When we make wrong judgments about things around us, we should know that whatever deduction or conclusion we must have reached about a particular thing in our lives, it is bound to be different from what others feel about that particular thing. What you consider perfect might be full of blemish to another.

All these are called value judgments. And they are one of the few things we have control over. Even if Stoicism pushes us to start thinking we have no control over everything in our lives (which is very true), it still points out happiness as one thing we have total control over. We have a right to be happy – truly happy. Even Epictetus agrees with this fact.

Secondly, your mind is your sanctuary, so train it perfectly, to withhold any condition. Stoicism agrees to the fact that life is hard, thus trying to train your mind while facing the world can be quite difficult. For example, it will be very difficult for someone who is putting himself through school and still trying to maintain a perfect mind. However, if one can achieve this feat, even while battling with everyday problems, then one is said to have attain the position of a true Stoic.

Also, take the life of Seneca as a guiding lesson. Seneca was rushed by a series of trial and obstacles. He was disgraced, exiled, lost lots of people that were dear to him, suffered as a slave, and was made to end his life by Nero. And when he knew it wasn't easy for anyone to follow virtue and goodness even in those situations, he stood his ground.

To this effect, Stoicism has made things easy for people that want to incorporate the principles in their daily lives. According to Stoicism pioneers, Marcus Aurelius and Seneca, it is easier said than done when following the core tenets of Stoicism. It is far bigger than just following the daily routines of your life.

Seneca had advised that in order to successfully incorporate and practice Stoicism in our daily lives, we should learn to start taking stock at the end of each day that passes. That way, you can jot down things that you don't even notice about yourself. You will be able to reflect on your mistakes and errors, becoming a better version of your self. For example, if you flare up unnecessarily at your subordinate, taking stock would make you assess that situation again and know if you are wrong.

Another way of incorporating Stoicism within our daily lives is one of the strategies used by the former Roman Emperor, Marcus Aurelius. Every morning, he would look up to himself and remind himself over and over again that no matter how hard he tried, he was bound to encounter difficult, stressed, ungrateful, impatient, annoying, and recalcitrant people every day of his life.

Therefore, this reflection he kept going through in advance would refresh his sense of reasoning and give him the patience he needed. He also acknowledged the fact that it is no fault of these people as they were also facing problems of their own. These problems were affecting them because of the way and manner in which their emotions ended up influencing their judgment.

Lastly, irrespective of how hard you think you might want to or try to influence nature, it's still going to be what it ought to be. In other words, accept nature and fate as your destiny. Accept the fact that if it is destined to be, then it will surely be. The world is way bigger than just our tiny little lives. Thus, we shouldn't hope to be the master of nature. Instead, we must accept whatever it throws in our way.

Expectations hurt in the long run, especially when we have put in too much hope. If we keep thinking "I pray it comes through," then it will never come through. But when we leave everything in the hands of nature, we do our best and leave the rest with the mindset of what will be, will be. We are indirectly preparing for the worst, which is a good sign for Stoicism.

Epictetus said, "If you expect the universe to deliver what you want, you are going to be disappointed, but if you embrace whatever the universe gives, then life will be a whole lot smoother."

Like we said earlier, this is just a piece of advice. But it is important to know that this advice is becoming relevant in today's world with lots of people trying to incorporate Stoicism within their daily lives.

Be that as it may, the storm will finally be over when stability and peace come into your life. Knowing the difference between what you can control and what you can't is the pathway toward peace. Now, guess what? Things will now start taking shape. You would be amazed at the way things will move from good to better.

A lot of us miss out on this bumper offer Stoicism offers us. When we hear the word Stoicism, many of us don't even know what it's all about. Our ignorance is really making us miss out on all the goodness this philosophy comes with. The previous chapters of this book must have laid emphasis on the freebies that are attached to Stoicism.

Nothing gives peace better than having control. Trust me - you will have peace of mind knowing that everything that surrounds you is under your control. In our everyday life, it has to do with one thing in general, one that encompasses every other thing; shifting focus from the end result, or things to the achievements that resides inside them. Instead of focusing on how good or bad our decisions are, we should focus on what they have achieved. That's the only thing that will keep us going.

For example, if you are putting together a catchy resume for a job promotion at your place of work, then you need to set your goals right. Focusing on the outcomes would not be advisable. There is a 50:50 chance that you might not get the Job. This is because the outcomes aren't in your control. However, you can choose to influence it - which still doesn't give you a hundred percent guarantee.

The best you can do is think of what you might want to achieve after bagging the job - the milestones you'd want to reach. This will give you the boost you need in writing a good resume. It is the Stoic way of doing things. Prepare your mind for both positive and negative outcomes, too.

Having control is the peace you deserve. It is far deeper than it sounds. The dichotomy of control has countless applications to everyday life, and all of them have to do with one crucial move; shifting your goals from external outcomes to internal achievements.

This will enable you to free yourself from any form of guilt or disappointment. It will give you peace of mind without any worries whatsoever. It is important to know that things don't always go the way we want. It's the wisest thing to do because even after we don't get the job, the best we can do is to forge ahead with our lives.

Shifting our focus from outcomes to achievements can help us keep some things in our lives under our control. That way, you will only focus on yourself with nobody to rival with at all. The only thing you will be competing with is making yourself a better version of what you were yesterday. Do this and you can be sure to enjoy nothing but a happy and serene life. Looking inwardly has also helped a lot of Stoics in keeping things under their control even when it seemed they were losing out.

Knowing what you control and what you don't is really not enough in getting the peace you deserve. Sometimes it takes much more than that to live a life of actual eudemonia. Mind you, the storm might be quite crazy to deal with in the beginning. Imagine someone going through a triple set back all at one time.

Let's say you lost a huge sum of money, your favorite pet ate poison behind you, and you lost your relationship with your boyfriend all at the same time. Now, that is one hell of a setback. Even the hardest of hearts between us would still melt at such a situation. However, after passing through the learnings of Stoicism, one would be surprised at how great you'd feel even after experiencing such a setback.

I know you must be feeling bad as we are reaching the last chapter of this book. I'm also sure you would agree with me that it been one hell of a ride since you started reading through this interesting book. Read through the next chapter as we put a lid on the top of our bottle of knowledge.

Chapter Fifteen

A New Dawn!

After the smooth ride, we've had together on the course of this book, I'm sure you would agree with me that something has changed in you – your perception toward living your life. There will be an urge for you to push yourself even further in achieving the goals you've set out for yourself. And remember - giving up is not an option.

Nothing like that exists in the Stoic dictionary. Immerse yourself with the kind of contentment and happiness Stoicism is going to bring you. According to many devoted Stoics, the new dawn that comes with practicing Stoicism is liberating and scintillating. Nothing beats that feeling of being free from unnecessary worry and serious emotions.

You now have your life in your hands. There is nothing anyone can say or do to intimidate you. Even if they try, they will eventually get tired and leave you alone. When you constantly start smiling over any tantrum they throw at you, when you start smiling at even their deepest taunts and tease, they will definitely back down.

Achieving this stage is not a day's job. At first, it might not look like your efforts are holding substance. But do not give up. The world today holds lots of temptations and events that may trigger our inner feelings into manifesting even when we never summoned them. For example, after reading a book on Stoicism and really wanting to practice the principles in our daily lives, you start getting tempted to break your resolve with something that is totally out of your control.

Being an alcoholic or womanizer could be a very hard thing to control. Irrespective of how hard we try, sometimes our inner feelings toward these vanities of life may end up overcoming our mind, body, and soul entirely. Imagine an alcoholic asked not to taste even a pint for a week; quite crazy, right? Or a womanizer tempted with a very beautiful woman and expected to look the other way.

It takes more than just a resolution on our part. We must be ready to let go of every urge to the vanities of this world. Let's adopt the mind of everything is given to us by nature and can be taken away by nature. Seneca cultivated this mindset towards living his life as a slave and nature eventually came through for him.

Let's learn to start expecting less from people around us. We should never forget that no one is perfect or even has total control of the things around them. One way or the other, we are all different parts of the same cosmos. Our everyday activities in life are a contribution to a much bigger world. Whether we do good or bad, it all has its own effect on nature.

Being a Stoic now makes one thing very clear; everything happens for a reason. If you don't believe that, then I urge you to start believing. Nothing happens on its own without the influence of another. If you are rich today, it's obviously because you've put in much hard work in order to turn out successful. Also, if you are a prominent and skillful footballer loved by all, it's because you have also put in much hard work while training in order to come out on top.

There is a light at the end of the tunnel for everyone willing to start a brand new life with Stoicism. Try it for a week and watch your world go smoothly. If you are depressed before, Stoicism is the fastest solution you can think of. The present-day settings of the world have made Stoicism relevant to the daily struggles of life. People now become stressed at work. The unemployed become depressed at home. Couples and relationships become strained. Lots of people end up losing focus and direction.

Living the life of a Stoic is not an easy path. Though it will build up one's lost confidence and self-esteem, it will make you feel different from the rest. For example, would you rather save up or buy steak every weekend? Would you rather visit your loved ones or go on a walk? Questions like these are hard to answer when you live like a Stoic. And of course, Stoicism entails making an emotionless decision. Thus, how do you tell if you are being influenced?

Stoicism might tidy up one's life, but it does leave some dots behind. But one thing it doesn't forget to do is give us contentment in the decisions we make. Believe me, if we stop thinking about death and just focus on our lives and making them better, we will move even mountains. We will surpass every obstacle like it's nothing. The only way to lead a good life is to train your mind perfectly.

That aside, you will now start becoming aware of your environment. You will also start paying attention to the things you control and the ones that are out of your league. This is very important to because it will hold the key to your new world. Let's take this example, no matter low our income or occupation may be, so long we are within the age bracket of 24-30, we might want to start doing things to live healthily and keep fit.

We might go to the gym to build our muscles. We might even go take a walk around the park to clear out head each time we feel stuffed. Do a little bit of yoga and meditate until our problems finally dissolve away. We do this not because we want to look good for the girls. Neither are we doing it just to attract attention from work or even accomplish our set out objectives. Instead, we are doing it for ourselves. Because we want to fulfill our urge toward leading a fulfilling life, irrespective of what anyone thinks.

That is an action of a true Stoic. Do not let the actions of others put you off. Do not let their actions control you. And do not let their actions influence your decisions and judgments. A true Stoic configures his or her mind to be indifferent from whatever feelings that may erupt inside.

Be that as it may, it is widely known that Stoics all over the world tend to attribute the qualities of a God to their founding fathers. They see them as an epitome of perfection, forgetting that they were also mere mortals like the rest of us. Marcus Aurelius, Seneca, and Epictetus were mere mortals that made mistakes, lived among people, loved and were loved by people, and in fact, they lost also like every other mortal.

Their attributes can be likened to our moments in life. The same way we have behaved in the course of our life is how they behaved. They'd shed tears when hurt. They'd cried when pained. They'd smiled when happy. The list is endless. Thus, they are very wrong in that assumption.

We are far from perfect. We also make mistakes, but one thing we can surely do is to walk our way through and make corrections to being a better version of ourselves. That and more are the reason why Stoicism came into being. However, the beginning of Stoicism wasn't to better mankind as a whole. It was actually a combination of their conversations, letters, medications, maxims, plays, diaries, and even notable events in their lives.

In moments of grief, they made sure they nursed themselves with their writings of strong will. In moments of obstacles and problems, they meditated their way through. They continuously tried making themselves better and better every day that passed in their lives. Therefore, can't we just be like that?

Why can't we strive hard and build ourselves back up each time we are down? Why can't we look up each time we are facing what may seem to be bigger and stronger than us? Why can't we soulfully meditate through our problems instead of sticking to alcohol and other social vices?

With that being said, practicing Stoicism perfectly doesn't need one to be a Ph.D. holder. As a matter of fact, there is little or no need for one to start writing crazy essays and books all in the name of practicing it. It is far from citing up words from the sayings of the early Stoics just to feel cool. It should be imbibed in our life.

It is also not a religion, it has no tenets that are grounded on the basis of religion. But it opens up our eyes to the possibility of living a life of absolute importance. This tenet had been upgraded and modernized from generation to generation. It had passed through reformation and transformation.

In the 20th century, there was low acceptance of the philosophy, but the 21st century gave rise to a whole new perspective as the philosophy gained popularity and recognition with lots of people applying it in their lives. To this effect, Modern Stoics have managed to tweak the principles so as to fit the settings of the modern world. And these tweaked principles make it more acceptable for people to enjoy and embrace the philosophy.

It has helped lots of people in finding a permanent solution to their problems. For example, let's say your friend had gone through one of the craziest and sensitive stage in his or her life. Imagine someone going through a double hurt. Losing a job and also losing one's parent (mum or dad) can be quite crazy. At that particular point in time, it will take every nerve in someone to hold his or her sanity.

Your friend would definitely not be the same again. Something must have changed in him or her. Something must have been broken in him or her. What can help is Stoicism. Stoicism will give that person a sense of reasoning. Stoicism will provide the strength to look the other way and carry on with his or her life. Stoicism will ensure you become strong - stronger than you can even imagine. It will teach you how to be good and see the world from a different perspective, thereby becoming happy.

Living in the new dawn of your life entails a few things and they are as follows;

1. **Eliminating Emotions:** This is something you must be familiar with at this point in time. It is one of the core principles of being a Stoic. If we can cultivate a mind where emotions can be overlooked, then we can proudly say that we have reached a stage of being a Stoic, thereby reaching eudemonia.

   Learn to control the mind. Learn to know what you can control and what you can not. Know the distinction between these two and everything will start working in your favor. When we feel angry about something that seems to be out of our control, we are only allowing these things or people get to us.

   However, we will also reach a point in the time of our lives where getting angry will be useless and unnecessary. In situations where anger used to be our only resolve, we will now start getting calm. This is when we've reached true Stoicism. Thus, the new dawn Stoicism will bring to our lives will be immense happiness and freedom from stress.

2. **Learn and Practice:** Learning is an everyday process. As the saying goes, no one knows it all. Thus, we strive to become better, every day of our life. Pick up a book or two about Stoicism. Ensure you immerse yourself completely in the

teachings and lessons. They might come in handy when solving a problem or two.

Don't get it twisted, learning is a continuous process. The same thing goes for Stoicism. As the world we live in today keeps changing continuously, the scholars of Stoicism keep reforming and making great changes to the principles of this philosophy so as to suit our world. Now, immerse yourself with the current state of things. Always know if there is any change. This can only be achieved when we keep learning every day.

Instead of staying glued and attached to just a particular type of information about Stoicism, why not get yourself immersed and updated with new formulations, knowledge, and scholarly ideas of Modern Stoics? These may come in different languages and training. To know is to forget and to practice is to remember.

3. **Accept Nature:** According to science, nature is orderly and regular. It is very organized and surrounds us with its beauty and mystery. Stoicism acknowledges the presence and supremacy of nature over us. Man and nature have a relationship which makes both of them connected, yet distinctive.

As Marcus Aurelius puts it when complimenting this perspective, "At every moment keep a sturdy mind on the task at hand, as a Roman and human being, doing it with strict and simple dignity, affection, freedom, and justice—giving you a break from all other considerations. You can do this if you approach each task as if it is your last, giving up every distraction, emotional subversion of reason, and all drama, vanity, and complaint about your fair share. You can see how mastery over a few things makes it possible to live an abundant and devout life—for, if you keep watch over these things, the gods won't ask for more."

4. **Living with Death in Your Heart:** We will all die someday. This perception will keep you on your toes. It will make you start thinking of how best to live your life. If you are always attending funeral services (we are not saying you should start attending funeral services), you would learn to understand and appreciate the true meaning of life.

Why waste your life doing things that won't give you the fulfilment you seek? Early Stoics have laid emphasis on this subject matter. This will show you that even those Roman thinkers always had it at the back of their minds that death is just a stone's throw away, thus, gearing them towards living a great life.

"Memento mori" is the mantra of all Stoics, thereby making them take the issue of death seriously. Thinking about death would make them remain focused on the principles and tenets to the philosophy.

But today, many people don't even want to spare a second thought for death. They obviously know that they will surely due someday, but they just don't want to picture themselves dying. Therefore, they end up spending large hospital bills, buying long life medicines, visiting Shamans, and even going on a meditation trip all in an attempt at prolonged life.

Meanwhile, their focus should be living a good and happy life for the time being.

5. **Know Thyself (Erecting an Inner Citadel):** We have raised emphasis on this part of Stoicism in the previous chapters. This is the first step to practicing Stoicism - the first thing to do when your mind is made up about following the path of Stoicism. We know our true self. No one knows us better than ourselves.

People can only get to us when we allow them in; when we show them the way to our mind. That is when they will spin their web of controversies and influence our decisions and judgments. We will be powerless as we will keep watching them without being able to raise a finger.

This is where looking inward and trusting yourself, knowing what you really want, is important, what you are really made of, and what you really seek in life. Build a formidable inner fortress that can not be penetrated no matter how much every variable working against you tries.

For instance, a man who had survived from a region where war, destruction, famine, and hunger dictates the days of his life would have developed a strong inner citadel which will be capable of holding him through any moment of his life. With the amount of chaos he faced, he had been able to look inward for a solution, thereby, becoming resolute, resonant, and totally indifferent from pain or pleasure.

Be that as it may, this brings us to the end of our esteemed book on Stoicism as a pathway to achieving complete happiness and peace. We will implore you to follow this path with much importance. This new dawn in your life is an opportunity for you to live your life appropriately. It is a second chance many don't even get at all.

Live well, stay happy, uphold virtue, and never allow your emotions to make the better part of your decisions and judgments. Do all this and you will be fine.

Conclusion

I'm afraid this is the end of this amazing and educational book which we believe had opened your eyes to the principles of Stoicism and its application to achieving complete happiness. I'm sure you would agree with me that Stoicism is one hell of a philosophy. Hard to maintain but very effective when applied.

And if you can maintain its application in your daily life, nothing can stop you from achieving all that you have set out to – well, except death, of course. This book has given you a new path to seek toward achieving what you feel is unachievable. Follow and tread the path steadily until it takes you to where your destination – eudemonia.

But rest assured, your perception of the world has changed. A lot of your buddies might start asking questions like, "what's happening, mate? Why the sudden change? Are you alright?" Such questions are bound to come, especially when you start applying what this book had taught you about Stoicism – eliminating emotions, being logical always, upholding virtue, and so much more. Do not let their comments deter you. In fact, if they conclude on parting ways with you, then so be it. They are obviously not the right circle you should be in.

The chapters of this book are outlined in a step-by-step format which should help you in understanding the philosophy of Stoicism even better. With lots of examples and real-life situations, we can refer back to it whenever we are facing or passing through a rough phase in our lives.

Never give up the fight toward being a better version of yourself. Continue to strive hard, the way Seneca and Marcus Aurelius, did even in tribulations. Immerse yourself with your situation. Accept it, whether good or bad. That is the only way you can move past it.

What you've gained from this book is a knowledge that can never be bought. Use it well, and help share with others if you can. You can even become a help to someone who needs it. Not everyone passing through a rough phase would want to voice out. Reach out to them and use Stoicism to heal them the way Seneca healed Lucilius.

And this brings us to the end. But, guess what? It's the beginning of a new dawn for you. As you are closing this book, you are opening the beginning of a new life with a fresh path. So the question remains, what are you going to do with this new light in your life? Throw it away? Or follow it until it fades?

Enjoy every day this new path brings forth. Live your life stoically like it's your last day as you apply the tips and ideas this book has offered you. And always remember, even when the enjoyment of living like a Stoic didn't immediately start manifesting, giving up is never an option for true Stoics. Thank you for sticking with us this far.

Good luck and God bless!

Emotional Intelligence 101:

Boost Your EQ For More Emotional Agility, Spirituality, Better Relationships, Success and Power - Achieve Mastery of Fear, Anger, Joy, Happiness, Persuasion and Social Skills

Introduction

To begin with, we all have at least an iota of this kind of intelligence in us, whether we acknowledge it or not. Emotional Intelligence goes beyond perceiving our emotions as a tool for making us weak. As a matter of fact, it is the total means of identifying, notifying, and making good use of our emotions to our own advantage.

It is important to know that a great deal can be gained from exploring our Emotional Intelligence. If we can tweak our emotions appropriately, we will not only be immune to a negative impact but also encourage success and growth in our lives. Many years ago, I was also a novice as regards this concept. In fact, I didn't know Emotional Intelligence existed at all. When I was mad and followed the dictates of my emotions, I didn't know I was blindly following my emotions.

I didn't know I was allowing my emotions to influence my decisions. Even when I was overwhelmed or extremely happy, I didn't know emotions could be quite detrimental in the decisions we make in the moment. But, when I came across a book that enlightened me about the world of Emotional Intelligence, I knew it was only a matter of time before I would start writing amazing content about it.

I knew it was only a matter of time before would I share my ideas on Emotional Intelligence with everyone around me. Well, we are here, aren't we? Emotional Intelligence deals with the ability to control your own emotions by having control of the outcome. Think about it - we really can't stop ourselves from the feelings that run through our body. These feelings are a result of our inner thoughts, wants, or desires, which are triggered by the outside forces.

So the question remains - if we cannot stop ourselves from feeling that way, what then can we do to manage those feelings? Emotional Intelligence is the answer you would always arrive at. Now, this is the message I bring with this book. What this book will do is to familiarize you with the values and principles, as well as tenets of Emotional Intelligence.

In the end, we will realize that our emotions will lead us astray most of the time. Whoever follows his or her emotions all the time ends up making a mess of his or herself. This is why great men always have a high level of Emotional Intelligence. Thanks to Emotional Intelligence, they can easily keep their emotions in check without the slightest issue. Believe it or not, a master of Emotional Intelligence is liked by all.

When you understand as well as respect others' emotions, you are bound to be loved. You are bound to be held in high esteem. A lot of these people around you will want to connect with you because they believe you are a great person with empathy and compassion. You will be able to build relationships and even earn the respect of everyone around you.

Be that as it may, read through the chapters of this book, so as to learn the real meaning of Emotional Intelligence. Allow me to take you through my journey toward becoming a master of Emotional Intelligence, as well as the outstanding benefits it has afforded.

Chapter One

What is Emotional Intelligence? (Definitions and Concepts)

It is important to know that the phrase "what is" contains lots of compelling ideas fused into one. "What is" does not only mean what defines a concept or an idea; it goes way beyond that. It encompasses scintillating and a wide range of thoughts concerning that concept or idea. Now, "What is Emotional Intelligence" is a very deep question. As a matter of fact, if we are to start delving into this question, the whole book won't be enough. Thus, we will be as concise as possible.

The question now is, "What is Emotional Intelligence?" We wouldn't be entirely wrong to we say emotions have been present since the beginning of time. Man was created to be clueless and emotion-free, until they ate the forbidden fruit in the Garden of Eden. Ever since then, man's eyes have been opened to the realities around him - and these new abilities of theirs came with emotions and feelings.

They now know their left from right. They bonded with their environment and could feel it. The first men started learning about the real meaning of emotions. Lots of questions had also gone through their minds; questions like why would they cry at a painful situation? Why would they feel happy when their purposes seemed to be fulfilled? Why feel anguish and grief when they lose someone close? These kinds of questions had been a mystery to them.

However, as time progressed, humans evolved. Emotions, over time, became better understood with lots of research, studies, and surveys carried out all through this era. In recent times, humans have mastered emotions to a large extent. Now, many people in the world today can easily tame their emotions, or show an expressionless demeanor even when battling with raging emotions inside of them.

The art of Emotional Intelligence can be said to be quite similar to Stoicism. With both synonymous to emotional control, one can boldly say that a true stoic is a master of Emotional Intelligence. In other words, both subject matters are intertwined and can be quite misconstrued for one another. Be that as it may, this book is all about Emotional Intelligence; thus, the focus will be given more to the concepts and definitions of that subject.

We can't fully delve into Emotional Intelligence without discussing emotions. Without these emotions, there would be no such thing as Emotional Intelligence. We need to have these emotions in order to make it possible for us to be able to measure and master them. There is no single person in the world without an iota of emotion in them. What differs is our level of indifference.

Meanwhile, the definition of emotion varies dependent on whoever is defining it. For example, an angry person might see emotions as the surge of innermost feelings which triggers certain hormones in the body as a result of outside circumstances. A calm person will tell you otherwise. Nevertheless, there are certain definitions which are quite accepted by all.

According to Sternberg, in his book, *In Search of the Human Mind*, "An emotion is a feeling comprising physiological and behavioral (and possibly cognitive) reactions to internal and external events."

In the same vein, Nairne posits that,

"An emotion is a complex psychological event that involves a mixture of reactions: (1) a physiological response (usually arousal), (2) an expressive reaction (distinctive facial expression, body posture, or vocalization), and (3) some kind of subjective experience (internal thoughts and feelings)."

Emotions are what we feel. They are independent and can hardly be controlled. For example, a temperamental individual would find it very difficult to control his or her anger no matter the number of hours spent in an anger management class. If the environment is not helping, then the classes would definitely have little or no effect on the individual.

Psychologically, emotions can be seen as a mental state where the mind translates our environment and outer circumstances into two possible outcomes – goodness or badness. Whichever outcome mind and body choose is exactly what we will feel. Let's take two quick examples, shall we? Our body responds to stimuli at the slightest touch. It's like our senses send a message to our brain, which in turn responds by making us feel the pain at the exact location of the touch.

If we get burnt by a fire while we are trying to drop a hot pot from the gas cooker, there would be a quick reflex between our hand and the pot. Thanks to stimuli, we would feel the pain exactly where we got burnt. That way, emotions of anger, pain, and probably sadness would set in as we would be left with a burnt hand.

In another example, a heartbroken person would definitely go berserk, becoming depressed and extremely sad. These are mostly the kinds of emotions that would rush in no matter how hard we try. With or without stimuli, these emotions are definitely going to show up. As James Averill rightly puts it,

"The concept of emotion . . . refer[s] to (1) emotional syndromes, (2) emotional states, and (3) emotional reactions. An emotional syndrome is what we mean when we speak of anger, grief, fear, love and so on in the abstract. . . . For example, the syndrome of anger both describes and prescribes what a person may (or should) do when angry. An emotional state is a relatively short term, reversible (episodic) disposition to respond in a manner representative of the corresponding emotional syndrome. . . . Finally, and emotional reaction is the actual (and highly variable) set of responses manifested by an individual when in an emotional state: . . . facial expressions, physiological changes, overt behavior, and subjective experience."

Be that as it may, what really is Emotional Intelligence? Like Stoicism, Emotional Intelligence is the ability to express, master, and control emotions. If you possess this quality, then you are definitely a master of emotions. You will be able to know and identify your emotions before and after you feel them. That way, you will be able to manage your emotions effectively and efficiently.

With Emotional Intelligence, getting angry unnecessarily, feeling stressed out or even depressed would definitely not cross your path. Emotional Intelligence would not only help you manage your emotions well, but also allow you to relate well by mastering the emotions of the people around you. When our best friend tends to read our emotions like the back of their hand, as ignorant as we might be, we call it sheer luck. Don't get it twisted - that friend might have been able to master emotional intelligence, thereby, making it very easy for them to predict your emotions even before they occur.

Salovey and Mayer defined Emotional Intelligence as,

"The ability to monitor one's own and others' feelings and emotions, to discriminate among them, and to use this information to guide one's thinking and actions."

In the same vein, Emotional intelligence refers to the capability of a person to manage and control his or her emotions and possess the ability to control the emotions of others as well. In other words, they can influence the emotions of other people, also. When you can easily place your hands on the mood of the people around you; when you can show them what true and genuine relationship actually means; when you can predict their behavior by focusing on their emotions. Then, you can call yourself a master of Emotional Intelligence.

Emotional Intelligence is a very broad subject matter that comes with at least four different fields of study. These can also be known as concepts, terms, or areas as the case may be. These are as follows:

1. **Self- Awareness:** This is the first step toward mastering your own Emotional Intelligence. This involves getting a grip of oneself as well as understanding our own emotions. When we are self-aware of our own feelings and emotions, then we are bound to make good choices as well as productive decisions.

Like true stoics, having control of our emotions would definitely shape us into a better man. I know you must be wondering how controlling your emotions would make you a better man. Yeah? Well, let's take Robbie for example.

Robbie is a 32-year-old doctor who works at a government renowned hospital. Before Robbie lost his wife, he was a very good doctor, probably the best the hospital had. He was fast with his hands, jovial with his patients, and nice to his co-workers. This is the real Robbie. Several months ago, he lost his wife to cancer, one of the deadliest diseases in the world today, and everything changed for Robbie.

Robbie blamed himself for not stopping what happened. He blamed himself for not being good enough. He blamed himself for everything. That way, he hit rock-bottom in his amazing career. Everything just went from bad to worse for him at home and work. He lost focus, he lost his confidence, and he lost his self-esteem. That is, until he came across the real meaning of Emotional Intelligence in a book he saw at a friend's place.

Robbie now understood how to control his emotions. He now understood that having self-control, self-awareness of your emotions, and self-esteem is the key to living a happy and fulfilled life. Like magic, his recovery was fast, smooth, and easy. Emotional Intelligence helped him dropped the guilt he had carried all by himself. Emotional Intelligence showed him light when he seems to have gotten lost. Emotional Intelligence shaped him into a better man.

This is the first step toward mastering your emotions. First, you need to accept them. Embrace them as they come. They are part of you - and as humans, we are definitely tied to them. If we get a call from a friend, we will definitely experience some emotions. If we are eating a plate of sweet pie, emotions will also come in. Even if it's just our morning walk, we will definitely feel emptions along the way. We are tied to it. We can't do without it. The best we can do is to acknowledge it, learn to live with it, and most of all, understand how to control it to our own advantage.

2. Self-Control: This is the second stage that comes after noticing and acknowledging our emotions. After accepting the realism revolving around our emotions, learning how to control it is the next best thing to do. Sometimes, when we feel pain in our body or heart, what normally happens next is the torrent of tears that will either wet our pillow or handkerchief. This is very normal, especially for ladies.

Sometimes, it is very hard for us to be able to control how we feel. Feelings can be like a raging bull when they need to be. They can also be as calm as a dove, too. It all depends on the circumstances revolving around you. But when these feelings surge rapidly, there should be something you can do to bring the levels down again almost immediately.

Some people hum a song; others just let it out by shouting at no one in particular. Irrespective of how you bring down your levels, what should matter is how well the method works. Controlling your emotions perfectly is like a wildcard to success in your endeavors. Take this, for example, when you are in a competition with a fellow competitor, all both of you will think of is the cutthroat decisions, like finding the weakness or loophole of your competitor.

This is very normal. But, controlling your emotions without allowing them to cloud your judgment would give you an upper hand. If your competitor hits hard at your weak area, taking the hit with a smile on your face would definitely unbalance your competitor. He or she would feel confused and disorganized. Now, that is your secret weapon – controlling those emotions. Thus, when you strike back, your competitor would definitely not see that coming.

Having self-control would help give you a clear head each time the need arises. Even amidst turbulent storms in your mind, and raging emotions, you would still have the confidence and assurance that you are on the right path.

3. Empathy: This particular type of feeling comes after learning how to control your inner feelings and emotions. Not everyone has this particular kind of Emotional Intelligence. Showing empathy to anyone around you is the desired trait that can only be fully harnessed after knowing yourself. If you know what your feelings are, notice them, and even control them, then you will definitely be drawn toward others.

You would be able to consider the feelings of others. When you understand people's emotions and feelings, you are sure to know what their next move is. You will be able to predict their actions even before they carry them out. It is very normal for a teenage girl to cry over heartbreak. Obviously, it could be her very first relationship experience and this goes a long way is shaping most teenage girls you see out there.

Many teens just don't know how to hold all those feelings inside of them. This is why you would notice a heartbroken teenager becoming a shadow of herself. If you understand people's inner emotions, you will be able to draw conclusions about any heartbroken teenagers after interacting with them. You will be able to place what they need, what they probably hoped for, and how you can actually come into the scenario.

Reading people's emotions comes to some as a gift. Unlike the rigorous training, exercises, and training others go through in order to become a master of Emotional Intelligence, some just find it very easy. Be that as it may, when you understand the emotions of the people around you, you will be able to interact with them even better. You will be able to know when to stop and when to apply pressure.

That way, the relationship you are preserving would even grow stronger by the day. Daniel was a 40-year-old man who lost all his money and assets in a bad stock market transaction. At the age of 32, he had his life all set out for him. He had a sweet family, a house he could call his own, his dream car, and a fat account balance. But his world went from white to black the moment everything came crashing down.

On a fateful Thursday, he had set out to end it all. His family left him, he lost his house, he lost his car, and most importantly, he lost his sanity. What saved Daniel was Emotional Intelligence. He had met an Emotional Intelligence expert before going to end it all. This expert sensed the raging emotions bottled up inside of Daniel. He followed Daniel secretly and quickly alerted the relevant authorities when he was about to take his own life.

Now, this makes me wonder, what would have become of Daniel if he hadn't spoken to an Emotional Intelligence expert? What if Emotional Intelligence hadn't been in existence? What if there was no empathy to begin with? This showcases the importance of Emotional Intelligence in our lives.

4. Social Skills: Just like empathy, social skill deals with using our Emotional Intelligence power to influence people's lives – not for the worse, but for the better. Don't get it twisted, Emotional Intelligence has been abused and used for evil purposes by some miscreants. Though it deals with understanding oneself and the people around you, it never promises to change one's beliefs and character.

This is the most advanced stage on the verge of mastering Emotional Intelligence, when we can understand the emotions of others around us and use this understanding to exert an influence in the lives of these people. With social skills, you will be able to know how to relate with everyone and anyone, thereby, carrying everyone along.

Social skills are an aspect of Emotional Intelligence that deals with the relation of one's emotion with another person's emotion. That way, you can both influence each other one way or the other.

With Emotional Intelligence, our lives are bound to be far better than they would be without it. When we apply it, we are surely setting our path toward greatness. We are definitely making ourselves into a better version of what we were yesterday. So, instead of allowing our emotions to dictate and influence our way of thinking, we should take control of Emotional Intelligence. The next chapter will look into ways of identifying and improving Emotional Intelligence. You don't want to miss it.

Chapter Two

Identifying and Improving Emotional Intelligence in Yourself and in Others Around You.

When things start falling into place and people start liking us in our personal lives or at work, it's not because we are special or unique. It's also not because we are better than the rest. It's because we have been exploiting our Emotional Intelligence. Emotional Intelligence is what has made us amazing over these years. And the funny thing about it is that some of us don't even have the slightest idea about this subject matter.

If only they knew the importance of this particular trait; if only they know it had been their inborn Emotional Intelligence qualities that had been working well for them; if only they know people liked them not because of what they have but because of how well they relate to and understand them. Then they would really know the true importance of Emotional Intelligence.

From Self-awareness to Self-control, Empathy, and Social Skills, Emotional Intelligence goes deeper than you can fathom. Now, the question remains: how can one identify Emotional Intelligence in oneself or even within others? It is important to know that Emotional Intelligence varies in every individual. We all can't have the same Emotional Intelligence Quotient. It surpasses one another.

Where some people can use this Intelligence to manipulate and influence other people's decisions, others can only understand the emotions running through a second party. When Daniel Goleman published a book as regards this subject matter in 1995, most people in the world had been very ignorant of the concept.

As a psychologist and a journalist in the field of science, he had taken a liking to the series of topics surrounding emotions, feelings, and emotions. He had always believed that human beings have a tendency of holding and staying in control of their feelings and emotions. He relates his theory to lots of examples, thereby showcasing how emotions had to be the henchmen behind our failures in life.

According to him, if emotions can be checked properly, then success will be the only song man will hear as the chances of being successful will be on the rise. Ripple by ripple, his idea moved from place to place, thereby changing the way people think as regards behavioral patterns towards emotions. If emotions can be checked, our behavioral pattern will definitely change for the better.

Like true stoics believe, emotions make one weak. They make one relax and chase nothing but failure and regression. When you are filled with emotions or allow your emotions to influence a very big part of your decision making, then you will find yourself making decisions that aren't even worth it. You will find yourself making compromises, all the days of your life.

So how do we really identify this Emotional Intelligence? How do we know we possess it? This is what this chapter will delve into. According to my own little understanding, I believe identifying Emotional Intelligence shouldn't be hard to pull off. To begin with, one needs to fully immerse himself with the subject matter and understand what the real meaning of Emotional Intelligence is. Now, here are the few points you should watch out for:

1. **Thinking About Feelings Almost All the Time:** This is probably one of the easiest ways to know and identify Emotional Intelligence in yourself. Like we pointed out in Chapter One of this book, the first stage to Emotional Intelligence is self-awareness, and this self-awareness deals with admitting to the fact that you have emotions running through you.

After this admission, a certain surge of emotions will start growing in you and you will now start having sober reflections. That way, we are bound to start thinking along with questions like: What are emotions? Why do we feel this way? Are they beneficial or detrimental? How can they influence my decisions for the better or worse?

These particular lines of thought will open up your mind to Emotional Intelligence. It will make you realize that Emotional Intelligence had been in you all along. What you should focus now on is how to really project this trait to the success of your everyday endeavors and that of everyone around you.

2. When You Think Before You Act: Many people in the world today lack this outstanding quality. This is why many of us end up making lots of regrettable decisions. Before we do anything, it's best if we first weigh the pros and cons of the decision.

That is the only way we can save ourselves from doing anything stupid or embarrassing ourselves in the long run. Its best we take a chill, sit back, and weigh our decisions before taking them. If you already possess this kind of amazing quality, then you are definitely intelligent emotionally without knowing it. This is also another way of identifying Emotional Intelligence in yourself or any other person.

3. When You Strive Continuously to be the Master of Your Own Thoughts: Even with the little or no experience you might have had as regard Emotional Intelligence, if you find yourself trying hard to hold your emotions together, even in trying moments, then you obviously possess this amazing trait.

It is important to know that emotions can hardly be controlled. We can't possibly control how we feel no matter how hard we try. But what we can actually master is our outburst towards these emotions. What we can really be in control of is how we react to these series of emotions that we feel. If the circumstances around us get us easily irritated and, as a result cause anger and frustration in us, what we can do to manage these raging emotions is properly manage our outbursts.

That way, you will be in charge of yourself. Instead of being a slave to your emotions, you will be in control of them instead. That way, your life will definitely take good shape and strike a balance that would make you thrive. In the end, it will create harmony between your core values and your objectives.

4.   Learning from Your Mistakes and Criticism: One thing that will help you identify Emotional Intelligence quickly in yourself or other people is the ability to pick up lessons from your mistakes and criticism. An ordinary person will normally feel bad when you criticize them heavily or lightly. Some might even give up totally after hitting a few stumbling blocks.

Someone with a high trait of Emotional Intelligence will not only thrive with criticisms but also ensure pick points from it. In fact, it is an avenue for self-development, self-reliance, and self-control. If these criticisms or mistakes don't get to you at all, then you are indeed intelligent emotionally. Instead of getting angry, you stay calm and learn from what was being said.

5.   Being Real at all Times: When you say things as they should be without sugarcoating them, you are intelligent emotionally. And it is important to know that these kinds of realists have few friends. It's quite unfortunate that a lot of people in the world today don't want to take things as they are. They don't want to accept reality no matter how you interpret it for them.

Emotional Intelligence focuses on reality. When you take things as they are, you hold your core values dear to your heart, and you don't give in to emotions, then you are emotionally intelligent. Be that as it may, you need to be steadfast and real at all times. That is the only way you can beat your emotions.

6.   Having Empathy: Empathy is one of the stages of Emotional Intelligence. When you possess this characteristic, then you are definitely good to go. What empathy does is to help you reconnect with the people around you. It will open up a pathway for a healthy relationship between yourself and the people around you. When empathy sets in, all you think about is the welfare of the people around you. You will be able to help them by understanding their emotions first.

When I say empathy, I don't mean compromises. Sometimes, we tend to mix up the meaning of empathy. Empathy doesn't make us weak or meek. Instead, it makes us compassionate toward the feelings of others. Together, all of you can understand each other and build a much better and more meaningful relationship.

7. Showing Appreciation and Acknowledgement: Emotional Intelligence is all about selflessness and understanding. It's all about leading a better lifestyle and one of the ways to make this happen is via appreciation and acknowledgment. When you show this trait to the people around you, when you shower them with praises for any good work they've done, when you show them how much you believe in them, then you are bound to be trusted.

With appreciation and acknowledgment, you will inspire the people around you. And guess what? It doesn't even cost a dollar. If one holds this trait, then that person is definitely intelligent emotionally. Praises boost the morale of anybody. Make this your keyword and you will build strong relationships with the people around you in no time.

8.   Being a Good Advisor: Only people that had mastered Emotional Intelligence can beat their chests to be good advisers. When you are completely free from the tricky hands of emotions, your words and decisions won't be influenced by them. Although being an emotional intelligence person will require you to be quite real with the people around you, the way and manner in which you present your words of advice should really matter.

In the verge of upholding your core values and principles, you can also be mild with your criticisms. When you present them well, it will only open up the hearts of people toward you. In other words, people will appreciate you more and even tell you more about themselves. When you see someone possess this attribute, then you know the rest.

9.   Being Apologetic When the Need Arises: The goal of Emotional Intelligence is to make sure you don't lose connection with the people around you. Being emotionally intelligent doesn't mean you are superior to the rest. It just means you are capable of controlling your outbursts and you possess the power over your emotions. Therefore, you are not too big to be apologetic when the need arises.

What most people didn't realize is that saying "I'm sorry," will never make you weak. Instead, it will make you become a more mature person. This is what people with Emotional Intelligence understand perfectly well. If you are like this or know someone who doesn't find it hard to say those words, then you've found Emotional Intelligence.

10.   Forgiving and Forgetting: Emotional Intelligence does not leave room for resentment or grudge. When you hold on to something that hurts, all you are doing is hurting yourself even more. It also means you are giving emotions a chance to lead you. When you hold on to something that hurts, it only means you aren't ready to move on. These emotions will definitely hold you down from progressing with your life.

But, when you forgive and forget, then you are giving yourself a chance to thrive. You are giving yourself a chance to see a new dawn. You are giving yourself a chance to see the light; a light that would lead to your peace of mind, prosperity, and plush.

Ways to Improve Emotional Intelligence

1.   Leave Your Comfort Zone: We never can tell what will happen to us if we don't even try out something new. Sometimes, the best way to improve or move forward is to challenge oneself with a new set of measures. When you test new waters, you open yourself up for new exciting experiences. This can only happen when you leave your comfort zone.

Emotions can be quite tricky. So when these emotions come, some people feel the best way to deal with these emotions is to avoid them. But, what is the assurance that these emotions will not come up again at a later date? Is this how we will be avoiding them when they come back? Why not look for a permanent solution by going outside your comfort zone.

Work toward a permanent solution. Face your fears if you have to. Make sure you hold yourself so as not to lose your way on the verge of finding a solution. No matter how shrewd it may look like, do not ignore your emotions. They may come back and bite you in the ass when you least expect it.

2. Know Your Triggers: Triggers are the factors that create a surge of emotions in us. Triggers can also be seen as conditions that create a tendency for us to feel emotional about certain circumstances. Thus, when you identify these triggers, your Emotional Intelligence will definitely improve for the better. You will know when and how to control your emotions even better.

When you know what your triggers are, you will be able to control the outbursts of your emotions. You would have been prepared beforehand before the emotions take you over. That way, your actions, decisions, and words will be controlled appropriately. When we have an idea of how our buttons work, only then will we be able to improve our Emotional Intelligence, if not entirely, at least to an extent.

In relation to outside forces, you will want to know why these outside forces become triggers and push your buttons. You will also want to know when they push your buttons. If noise is what irritates you, especially when you are trying to work, read, or even listen to something important, then you should adjust it.

3. **Not Making Decisions in a Bad Mood:** This is a very bad thing to do, especially when we make hasty decisions when we are angry or frustrated. These situations cannot be totally avoided. But, that doesn't mean we should fall into the trap. When we are in this bad mood, we should learn to be calm and collected.

After which we can make our decisions when we become sober. Someone who makes decisions out of anger or frustration will only be visited with one outcome, and that is regret. When we are in a bad mood and our emotions tend to get the better of us, we lose focus and sight of the good side that lingers.

When we are constantly living in a bad mood, when we start feeling irritated at every little thing that comes our way, either at work or at home, then it will be very helpful if we refrain from making decisions. Because these are decisions we might regret when we start becoming sober. So when we stop this act, we will definitely improve our Emotional Intelligence.

4. **Making Decisions in a Good Mood Should be Avoided, Too:** I know you might be surprised about this point, but believe me; you won't want to make decisions in a happy mood either. There is always a tendency for you to say or do things you aren't even capable of doing when you are extremely happy. Zed took his family to a football game on Saturday afternoon and luckily for him, they won the match in a grand style.

This made Zed very happy and he decided to take his children out on a treat to the only expensive resort available in the town. Unfortunately, he had very little in his pocket. What he has can't even take the kids to an average resort, let alone an expensive one. But, out of genuine happiness and thrill, he made a decision he can't really uphold.

Now, if you know this is the kind of person you are, then I would advise you to always keep your mouth shut each time you are happy. This would save you from getting yourself into more trouble or even embarrassing yourself in the long run. We should always learn to be conscious of our actions and deeds.

5. **Hold on to Your Core Values No Matter What:** Along the line, we tend to start out beautifully well with our newfound Emotional Intelligence. But, along the line, circumstances and events happening in our lives will continuously make us reach a breaking point. For example, the stress at work might be becoming too harsh, friends and family might become too demanding, and life as a whole may become quite challenging.

When you lose your values and principles, you tend to become a shadow of yourself. That is when we would advise you to start thinking back to when you found yourself. If we've lost that touch with our inner self, all we need to do is to reconnect with it. That is the only way we can rediscover ourselves. When we hit a setback, we should go back to our values and principles; they are the only cushion we can fall back on.

That makes it a wrap with the various ways of identifying and improving your Emotional Intelligence. All you need to do is to look inward and find these outstanding qualities in yourself. Believe me - we all have these qualities in us, at least some, if not all. If only we can learn to make good use of them, our Emotional Intelligence will improve beyond measure.

Chapter Three

Secrets to Boosting Your Spirituality and Tapping into an Endless Amount of Joy

Spirituality comes with an open mind. It comes with a mind that is devoid of emotions, feelings, and unstable conditions. In the course of our lives, there are certain occasions where things seem to be going south, where everything and anything we engage ourselves in end up being unsuccessful, where our most cherished relationships end up getting sour as we lose that connection with our friends and family.

In the same vein, we may be forced to withdraw into our shell. We may be forced to be a shadow of ourselves. Instead of being the ever-smiling and carefree lady or gentleman many had known us to be, we start becoming something different simply because we've lost that touch with happiness and joy in our lives. Now, this is where Emotional Intelligence comes in as a way of boosting your spirituality into reaching your inner self. That way, you will become a better version of yourself in no time.

Racheal had been a straight-A student right from her pre-college days. Racheal would even go on to tutor many of her colleagues because she was that good. Many referred to her as the female Albert Einstein of their time. This academic prowess brought lots of joy and happiness into the lives of Racheal and her family. But everything turned when she lost her dad after taking her final exams. She lost the focus and the joy she derived from being an academician.

Her dad was her inspiration and support. The moment her dad died, she felt the need to quit. Not until she came across this the concept of Emotional Intelligence as a method of boosting one's spirituality. There and then, she knew all she needed to do was to find herself, again. She knew all she needed to do us to go back and meditate until she opened her inner chakras. That was the only way she could be free from any form of anger, sadness, guilt, and regret. And it worked like magic. She got into college and has been acing her exams ever since.

Now, when I say spirituality, I'm not talking about the voodoo kind of spirituality, in case your mind starts wandering toward that direction. Instead, I'm talking about following a pathway which will lead to a better version of what you were yesterday. It is important to know that achieving this feat doesn't come easy at all. In fact, you will need to put much work, dedication, and commitment into it for it to work. You will really need to let go of the things that are tying you down.

For example, you can't suddenly want to start meditating with a heavy heart. You and I know that is not possible. For meditation to work effectively and efficiently, your heart needs to be free. You will really need to drop any connection or attachment you have with the world. That is the only way you can reach your inner self. This is where Emotional Intelligence comes in. If Emotional Intelligence teaches you to control your outbursts and keep a check on your emotions, don't you think your spirituality level is going to increase? Don't you think you will be able to find yourself and at the same time connect with the people around you even better?

There are lots of benefits attached to Emotional Intelligence. All you need to do is just open your eyes to the possibilities around you. When you have an improved relationship with your co-workers at your place of work, you will thrive at your place of work with many people watching after you. When you have a good connection with the people at home, it means you have people to fall back to and that would result in joy and happiness.

And if ever you start getting a surge of emotions that would be too much for you to handle, the best thing to do is to stay calm at that particular moment. If possible, meditate for a while. This will really calm your emotions. But, if you lost your values and principles along the line as the emotions may seem to have taken over, spirituality will help you regain the lost balance and stability in your life. It will help you see past those emotions, no matter how shrouded they might be.

Kane, who was supposed to be promoted to the position of a Junior Partner in his law firm, woke up one morning with joy and happiness in his heart. He knew this was definitely going to be his promotion. He knew this was definitely his day and he was well prepared for it. He had gotten the right tuxedo, the right shoes, and the right tie. But unfortunately for him, Emily was given the promotion instead. You can imagine the hurt on Kane's face as he felt his world crumble right in his presence.

This stunt affected Kane a lot and made him sad all throughout the week. Like a snail, he regressed back into his shell. He lost his cheerfulness, his joy, and his charisma along the line. But with spirituality, he gradually found his way back to being happy and ecstatic. It wasn't an easy journey for him, but in the end, he was able to found his way back. This was only possible because he was able to let go of his covetousness and his attachments to this world, and control of his outburst.

Now, you can be like Racheal and Kane. You can control your emotions and manage them effectively with spirituality. When you feel lost and sad, you should always remember that there is a pathway which you can follow to reach happiness and immense joy. That pathway is spirituality. Ripple by ripple, you will find yourself growing and building a stronger connection with your inner self. Your values and principles would now be your guiding angels.

Additionally, it is important to know that we can try lots of techniques and ways toward reaching our inner selves. Whichever one that works for us should be our own special technique. You shouldn't copy others by following their ways. What if their ways don't even work for you? Also, you should know that what has worked for you over the years might now work for you again. So, it is vital for you to be highly flexible towards reaching your inner self.

You can also try out any old forms of spirituality that you can think of, no matter how traditional they may seem. What should matter is how effective and efficient they seem. If it helps you concentrate and foster your journey to the other realm, then I would advise you to keep doing it. Achieving growth, stability, and balance in one's life is not a small thing to do. In fact, it can be quite tricky at times. One minute, you might be making progress and the next, you will just realize how stuck you had been. This is where versatility comes in.

Now, what will this chapter do? This chapter will enlighten you on the connection between spirituality and Emotional Intelligence. It will delve into the working relationship between both subject matters. If in the end, you still can't find the answers you are looking for, then we would advise you to stick with us through the remaining chapters. This book will definitely hold answers to your overall questions and mysteries.

Your spirituality journey is your own. Whatever you do to make it amazing is really up to you. When you start feeling pains, hurt, sadness, and even regret, what you need to do is to start going spiritual. If ever everyone rejects you, your inner self is always there to embrace you and show you your true self. Go back to it and make peace with yourself. It is only after making peace with yourself that you can make peace with the rest of the world. So, how do you strengthen your spirituality, I'll tell you.

1. Forgiveness: There is no better way to achieve ultimate peace. When you forgive, you are letting go of the heavy load on your head. When you forgive, your heart becomes lighter. This is the first step towards making a change in our lives. With lots of bad things that are taking place in this part of the universe, there is only a little or no chance at all that we might end up hurting someone or being hurt by someone either intentionally or even unintentionally.

Whichever way the case may be, we shouldn't hold on to such a negative feeling. Trust me; it does no good at all to hold a grudge against someone for a long time. Whether we like it or not, a grudge will only harden our hearts and make us look extremely bad in front of others. In the end, we will not even be able to concentrate fully at work, at home or with friends. That way, our connections with friends and families will end up getting strained. This is not what we want for ourselves.

Spiritually, a hardened heart cannot connect with his or her inner self. This is a vital rule that guides all spiritual levels. You need to be sure that your heart is completely free from hate and grudges in order for you to connect with your other side. Thus, we would advise you to practice forgiveness every blessed day of your life. Seek out those who have trespassed against you. Forgive them even if they don't act like they need forgiveness. This will only save you additional stress.

2. Honesty in Words and Deeds: One thing we shouldn't forget is that an honest heart has nothing to hide. When we are honest with our friends and family, no matter the circumstances, we are opening a path to a stronger connection. When our heart is free from lies and dishonesty, our spirituality level automatically rises. Thus, when you are honest in words and deeds, you will never lose that connection with your true self.

Accept your flaws and shortcomings. If you are wrong, admit it to others. If you err against anybody, go and apologize to them. Always keep an honest relationship. When we start shading our dealings from our friends and families, suspicion starts to arise. That way, there will be no connection at all and the little we have preserved will eventually fade away. If we start learning the true meaning of honesty, we will realize that telling another your deepest fear, your inner secret, and your flaws won't make you little.

Instead, it will show how much they can trust and believe in you. It will only tell them the extent to which they can connect with you. So, go out with your friends, invite them over for dinner if possible, and let go of every standard you have set for yourself. Expectations and standards will only make you become too stiff and stagnant.

You can even organize a support group. If you don't have the means to organize one, then you can simply attend one with family and friends. In case you start feeling shy, there are many support groups where your identity is not even required. Feel free to join. You will realize that support groups can be very helpful, too. You can also get attached to a spiritual leader. Make him/her your role model. They will gladly show you the path to follow in terms of honesty. Spiritual leaders always have a tendency to listen. Don't hesitate to pour out the hurt.

3. Reach Your True Self: We alone know ourselves and we are each unique in our own way. When we start feeling bad or drifting off from our purpose in life, there is a need for us to come back to shape and one of the best ways to do that is to explore our inner self. When we explore our inner selves, we are reaching out to the real parts of us that had stayed locked inside of us, the real side of us that completes us.

When we are true to ourselves, we are creating a life of plush, peace, and stability for ourselves. When we explore our real selves, we are directly or indirectly boosting our spirituality. That way, only immense joy, and happiness will await us at the end of our journey. Now, how do you explore your inner self? It's pretty simple.

To begin with, you can start by writing down important moments in your life. Write about the challenges you've faced and how well you overcame them. If you do this well, you will be able to use this writing as your guiding points and principles in your future endeavors. You can also be mentored by a spiritual leader. They would be able to fill you in as regards your self-exploration. You can also follow the path of meditation. This can only work with enough focus. In the end, you will be able to reach your true potential spirituality.

4. Value Your Principles: At the end of it all, our principles and core values are all we've got. They are the guidelines that we should follow in order to reach the peak of our spiritual growth. Our principles should be our knight in shining armor. They should hold our thoughts together and make us focus on what we really need to do. Make your principles your rules, and life would fall into place. However, there are circumstances that may warrant us to skip these principles.

When this happens, you don't have to beat yourself up too much about it. It's true our principles are the lights that shine our pathway to balance and stability. But, it is not true that skipping the principles once will make us lose our connection. Principles should be flexible. They should be able to fit into the current situation of things. That way, we will be able to adjust ourselves easily when the need arises.

5. Understanding Spirituality Itself: Spirituality itself is a very broad topic. We need to first understand what it really means before we can decide to delve into it. With lots of people making up misconceptions about the subject matter, we would advise you to find a well-accepted definition and meaning. That way, you can be able to interpret spirituality in your own terms.

So, what do you need to do after understanding the concept of Spirituality in your own terms? It's pretty simple. We would advise you to reflect on it. Think deeply about how spirituality can take you to exactly where you want to be. Think of how it would help you boost your level of spirituality. If you want, you can write them down, too. When you really understand something properly, you will be able to tweak it to your own preference.

6. Your Body is Your Temple; Take Care of It: The body is the vessel that holds the mind and the soul. Without a perfect and well-conditioned body, there would be no spirituality. It is important to know that both the body and the mind are connected in the sense that one can't function aside from the other. In other words, always take good care of your body. That is a way of boosting your spiritual levels.

So, the question now remains, how can we really care for our body in order to maintain a healthy lifestyle? First and foremost, you need to eat well. A balanced diet should always be maintained in order to support a healthy body. Secondly, sleeping well is also very important. When you don't sleep well, your body will definitely not feel right. Then lastly, you need to exercise occasionally. Then you exercise the body and keep fit, you are only inviting a healthy body. If your body is sound, then reaching the peak of your spirituality shouldn't be hard to pull off.

Thus, you need to find out which one works well for you. What works for your friends might not work for you. This is why you need to figure out what your preferences are. Stick to those preferences and your body will be just fine.

7. Relate with People of Like Minds: When you move with people who are far higher than you spiritually or people that will always like to scale higher in terms of their spirituality, then there is a very high chance of you improving your level of spirituality. If you are always with people like this, it will be easy for you to connect with them spiritually. Aside from these connections, it will also be very easy for you to seek out corrections and new ideas on how to approach or boost your Spirituality.

Together, you can reach out to more people, thereby connecting with even more people than you had earlier imagined. You can form a group or even join one to be with these people. You can share ideas, argue out assumptions, and reach a necessary agreement if the need arises. There is always an advantage to that particular kind of group. Imagine the positive vibes you will feel when the group connects spiritually.

Well, there you have it. It's no longer a secret. These are exactly the same secrets lots of these so-called masters of Emotional Intelligence won't tell you. Immerse yourself in it, devote yourself to it, and make sure you follow it to the letter. The rest will play itself out. The next chapter promises to be more exciting and entertaining - trust me.

Chapter Four

Proven Emotional Intelligence Strategies to Drive Your Success, Power, and Motivation

In life, we all have to subscribe to different strategies if we truly want to lead a life we can be proud of. These strategies can be long cuts or short cuts. They can be negative or positive. They can be anything at all. But one function they all perform perfectly is to make sure we reach our goals or objectives. If you are a stockholder, there are strategies which you have to employ in order not to lose out in the stock market. If you are an entrepreneur, there are also cutthroat strategies you need to make use of in order to stay at the top of your game.

Be that as it may, you can't reach a milestone in life cutting out strategies to use. These strategies will serve as the guiding principles toward achieving that goal in life. Now, as regards Emotional Intelligence, what are these strategies that would ensure your Emotional Intelligence continues to improve day in and day out? What strategies are there to employ for you to be able to reach the peak of your Emotional Intelligence? What strategies would you employ in order to achieve remarkable levels of motivation, success in your career, and the immense power of your emotions?

To begin with, many people have found it quite unnecessary to engage themselves in these strategies. This is because technology today has evolved to the extent where intelligence can be tested in no time. The IQ quiz can explain our level of intelligence in no time. That way, if a person whose IQ is quite high took the test, he or she might be subjected to start thinking testing the Emotional Intelligence would be quite unnecessary. After all, their IQ is very high, thus, their Emotional Intelligence should also be high.

Now, this is a very wrong notion. You can have a very high IQ but end up with a very low Emotional Intelligence. The ability to think fast differs from the ability to control emotions. They are two different things entirely. According to some group of scholars, they see Emotional Intelligence as the, "capacity to be aware of, control, and express one's emotions, and to handle interpersonal relationships judiciously and empathetically."

Now, do you still think Emotional Intelligence is irrelevant? Do you think your IQ alone would make you a better person? If your mentality has changed, then welcome to the world of Emotional Intelligence. But, if you are still thinking in the same line, then I would recommend you follow the next chapters. That way, you will definitely find the answers you seek. Be that as it may, it is important to know that we live in a world of interactions - or should I call it globalization.

We live in a world where interactions become a must for us as individuals living under the same cosmos. So, how would you maintain these relationships and connections if you don't even know the real meaning of relationships and connections? This is exactly what Emotional Intelligence would add to your horizon. It would show you the possibilities around you, thereby fostering your relationships and connections as well as helping you reach your inner self.

Trust me; you can only reach your true potential when you know yourself. When you immerse yourself with the idea of who you truly are, that is the only time which you will be able to move forward. In the end, you will feel inspired by every day setting out easy and perfect. That is the only time where you will get motivated, inspired, and achieve ultimate success.

Over the years, Emotional Intelligence has been gaining momentum, with top companies of the world adding the concept to the list of important values and virtues they need before employing new hires. With time, it has moved from the personal skill people use to reach their inner self, build, and maintain relationships to professional skills people seek out before making a hire. If you are wondering what Emotional Intelligence has to do with being professional, then allow me to break it down for you.

As an important skill in professionalism, Emotional Intelligence will allow the workers to remain professional no matter the circumstances they find themselves in. If we can master our own feelings and emotions at work, we will be able to keep everything professional. We have heard of cases where employees make out at work or even after work. This unprofessional act may come to bite the firm deep in the ass if fast measures aren't taken. But, with Emotional Intelligence, the tendency for that particular kind of stunt to happen would be close to zero.

These raging feelings would be kept in check and any form of the unprofessional act would be discouraged entirely. Emotional Intelligence would further encourage empathy for others around you, self-awareness for your own emotions and feelings, and the right motivation that would enable you to keep a straight head at work or at home. To cut it short, Emotional Intelligence leads to professional alertness and efficiency. It would also open up our mind to the performance of our friends and family.

So what is this chapter all about? This chapter will familiarize you with these well-known and well-trusted strategies of Emotional Intelligence to open up a new pathway for motivation, success, and immense control over your emotions. Now, what are these strategies? There is only one way to find out, yeah?

1.   Trusting Your Intuitive at all Times: One thing we should never take for granted is our intuition or "gut." According to popular research carried out many years ago, it was agreed that our intuition is a signal or warning our true self sends to us when the need arises - and they are hardly wrong. You should know that your gut is an effective and efficient tool that should be used to your advantage adequately. Do not neglect it for no just reason.

To all rational thinkers, intuition is a very important part of their decision-making process. They never joke with what their gut tells them. If harnessed properly, this can be a very important tool for you to achieve complete success, power, and motivation in your life. Be that rational thinker. Always trust your intuition. When you start feeling odd about a particular person or project, do the needful. Take the necessary step so as not to end up with regrets.

That way, we would only end up making better decisions about our lives, using sound judgments about our professionalism, and improving our Emotional Intelligence. You will come to realize that you were missing out when you did not trust your intuition.

2. Quiet the Mind if You Can: Now in cases of too much brouhaha, this strategy can come in handy for you if you know how to use it. And if you don't, I would suggest you learn it. Learn to shut everything out of your mind. And when I refer to everything, I'm talking about the noises, the stress, the arguments, and so much more that would hinder you from concentration. If you cannot manage it, then just shut it out.

That is the only way you will be able to think properly and accurately. Most people end up losing focus when they are stressed, tensed, and in a situation where noises are just too much. There is no way you would be able to think rationally or even communicate clearly in this state. Thus, if you don't have the ability to shut everything out, then we would advise you to walk away from that place. That is the only way you would be able to think properly.

But if you can clear your mind even amidst the stress around you, then that is just perfect. This strategy would come in handy because it would help you accelerate your rate of thinking rationally. You can easily slip into meditation during that time. It would help you keep the focus on what to do. In the end, your Emotional Intelligence would improve greatly, and this improvement would lead to motivation and success.

3. Know that you are Different from Your Emotions: This is the first step to greatness. The moment you establish the fact that you are not your emotions, you will move forward. That is when you will realize that nothing can stop you from realizing your dreams. When we start having the notion that our emotions lord over us, that is when we have finally accepted defeat.

Don't get it twisted; feeling the streams of emotions running through us is what makes us human. Just because you don't want your emotions to lord over you doesn't mean you should start forcing yourself on not feeling anything for. Even if that is possible, it is not right. Feelings and emotions are natural circumstances we cannot stop. We can only control the way we react. Thus, instead of depriving yourself these emotions, you should concentrate on controlling how you react. Then, start by knowing your emotions don't make you who you are. You are not your emotions.

4. Be Optimistic at all Times: This is one of the strongest tools that you can use to achieve motivation, success, and power. Optimism comes with a clear mind. A troubled mind cannot be optimistic as their hopes will be shrouded by fear, uncertainty, and frustration. As someone who is emotionally intelligent, you should be optimistic. That way, you would be able to place optimism in the right situations and circumstances.

But before you do that, ask yourselves these questions: Are you the kind of person who just sees things as they should be or believes there is more to it than meets the eye? Are you the type of person that doesn't see things differently from being a combination of 100% sheer luck and 0% practice? Are you the type of person that believes things happen as they should, thus leaving no room for blame? If you are, then you really need to practice being optimistic more often. When you are optimistic, it inspires and motivates you to reach great success.

5. Your Ego is Your Downfall; Kill It: Ego is the number one enemy to man right from the inception. Our ego had always been the cankerworm that eats our whole being. It stretches out to how we react to the situations and circumstances around us. It takes over our decision making. In fact, it is present in every step of our lives. Now, the best way to reach our peak is to forgo our ego. When we let go of our ego, we will be shocked at how things would play out differently than we had earlier anticipated.

It is important to know that no one can make you feel inferior or awful about yourself if you don't give them the power to. If you let yourself feel less than what you are, that is the only way they can make you look inferior. According to a study on ego, it was concluded that ego is the beginning of every downfall. If our ego is in the way of our success, we would definitely not make progress.

Additionally, there is no place for ego in Emotional Intelligence. As a matter of fact, you can't be filled with ego and at the same time claim to be a master of Emotional Intelligence. When you are filled with ego, your inner self stays far away from you. There will be no connection at all so long you still harbor ego in your heart. So start by killing off your ego. Happiness and success will definitely follow suit.

6. Embrace Your Emotions: This strategy also works perfectly. Understanding your emotions perfectly is one of the tenets of Emotional Intelligence. But, acknowledging them as they come would definitely improve your Emotional Intelligence, thereby fostering motivation, success, and power to control the outcome of your emotions. Unlike many people that would prefer to just neglect or even look the other way when these emotions come, accepting and acknowledging them is the best way to do it.

When you accept, understand, and at the same time acknowledge these emotions, you are definitely going to find emotions that are going to be of good use. Don't get it twisted; these emotions can come in two ways, good or bad. But what should matter is our ability to use and manipulate them for the better. If we can understand our emotions properly, we will be able to use them for our own good. There and then, motivation will set in, paving the way for success.

7. Think Before You Speak: Sometimes, our emotions end up carrying us away so much that we end up not knowing exactly what we have just spewed out from our mouths. For example, when certain expectations aren't met, we tend to start feeling frustrated and tensed, thereby, using our mouths to say things we don't even mean. The reason we make these mistakes is that we hardly think before we talk or act in cases like these.

Additionally, when these expectations are met beyond our imagination, we tend to start feeling ecstatic and extremely happy, thereby, ending up saying things we can't even do. This is very common when people end up getting what they want or even achieving success in their endeavors. If only we can think before we speak even in the happiest and saddest moments, then we would realize that everything won't look so complicated in the long run.

Let's find a way to conceal our emotions. And if we cannot do that, then let's make sure we don't utter a word all through the phase. Our words are the true reflection of our hearts. We should learn how and when to use them appropriately. Now, how do you maintain this? It's simple. You can get attached to someone you can trust. That way, you can let out anything you have in you before you end up exploding. Afterward, you will feel light. We end up making these mistakes with our words because of the baggage we carry.

8. Imagine yourself to be Someone Else: Instead of judging others from afar, how about you go close to them or, better still, try wearing their shoes to see where it pinches? According to a popular saying, "What turns out to be a 6 to you might be a 9 to me." This doesn't mean we are both wrong. Instead, it's just our perspective that differs."

Instead of seeing ourselves as perfect, how about we try seeing things from others' perspectives? If we start thinking that our thoughts, decisions, and opinions are always right, then there will be no room for development and improvement at all. We will be stuck in our own world without even realizing it. Let's try and give others a chance to explain their own opinions.

Let's hear them out too and observe their points. You may be shocked at how wrong you have been all along.

Be that as it may, whenever you try to boss over anybody or impose your decisions on them, take a few minutes to hear them out. Listen to their perspectives. Try and put yourself in their situation so as to have a deep understanding of their notion. This is the only way to foster a healthy relationship with the people around you. When you always try to listen to yourself all the time, your connection with them gets severed and strained.

9. **Law of Attraction:** There is no better way to achieve complete motivation and success than to believe in the law of attraction. When you believe that what comes around actually goes back around, then there is nothing stopping you from desisting from doing negative things to the people around you. Remember, what you reap is what you sow. Thus, wouldn't you rather sow goodness?

When you think of only good, then success will definitely come knocking at your door. When you think better, happiness will also become part of you. That way, your journey to the other side of you will always be smooth and easy. Believe it or not, karma is real. And when it comes knocking, you won't even expect it. This is why you should always treat people right no matter what the circumstances.

10. **Always Give Others a Listening Ears:** According to Mahatma Gandhi, we should, "speak only if it improves upon the silence."

These few words should be coated in gold as they hold great meaning. When you are a good listener, you are definitely making it easy for the other person to feel free in continuing his or her conversation. Quality listening gives the other person confidence in what he or she is saying. Even if what the person is saying doesn't add up, allow them to finish making their point before you interrupt. Stopping a person halfway in a conversation doesn't really go down well with some people.

Thus, give the listening ear to anyone that needs it. It's another way of fostering your relationships with the people around you via Emotional Intelligence. In the end, you will be able to derive motivation from the things you've heard, the things you've been able to digest, and the things you feel would be useful later.

There you have it. Do you want to succeed so badly in your endeavors, but have been faced with so much defeat, you're about to give up? Do you need motivation as regards your business or relationships? All you need to do is to follow the tips I'd listed above. Trust me - everything will change for the better in no time.

Chapter Five

How You Can Boost Your Emotional Intelligence Almost Overnight

In the previous chapter, we looked into the effective and efficient strategies one can use to boost Emotional Intelligence and also to reach a good level of motivation and success in life. In as much as Emotional Intelligence is concerned, you cannot lead a good life without a touch of it. Either intentionally or unintentionally, you just have to exude true Emotional Intelligence in order for you to be truly happy in the end.

As a trending topic in the United States of America, there has been a call for the introduction and development of this subject matter in the society at large. The government now believes Emotional Intelligence is the backbone to leading a happy life and a happy individual life equates to a happy society. If the people of a particular region or geographical location are happy, there will be little or no hindrance to the policies of the government. That way, the government can achieve its policies and the people will also remain happy.

No matter how you look at it, Emotional Intelligence provides a win-win situation. If you are a master of Emotional Intelligence, very little will get to you; that is, if they get to you at all. You will be in control of your tempos and your push button would definitely be in your own hands. Where your intellectual ability gives you the avenue by which your thinking rate would be very fast, Emotional Intelligence provides you with an avenue where your levels of emotional outburst, relationships, connections, and spirituality remains at their best.

Be that as it may, a lot of people have asked quite a whole lot of vital questions about Emotional Intelligence over the past few years since it became a trend in the American society. As a novice or beginner to the world of Emotional Intelligence, it is very normal for you to start acting funny and all worked up over nothing. Even the Stoics still finds it hard to manage and keep their emotions in check, let alone a normal person with no philosophy at all.

Thus, don't push yourself. Feel free to ask those that are more knowledgeable than to you in this line of discussion. Remember, he who asks never loses his way. You can ask how much time it will take for one to be a complete master of their emotions. You can also ask when one can actually master the control of their emotions. You can equally ask if someone can build up this outstanding trait overnight. Feel free to test all boundaries. It's better to know what you are about to enter before even making a move.

Now, if you are seeking answers revolving around Emotional Intelligence, then this book is the right book for you. But if your questions are revolving around gaining this Emotional Intelligence trait overnight, then this chapter is a must read for you. Moussa, who was an immigrant from Syria due to the war that had ravaged his home, came into the United States of America with the hope of starting afresh, with the hope of getting greener pastures.

As a Muslim and an Arab, the society didn't actually welcome him with open arms. Every day that passed, he was treated with disdain and discrimination. Quite a lot of people in America hold the view that these immigrants are nothing but miscreants who have come to take up jobs meant for the real Americans, thus the cold treatment Moussa received from the people around him. No matter how hard he tried to make friends, they just weren't into him.

His Middle-East accent and religious background gave him up no matter how hard he tried to blend in. But the big question Moussa had to answer was if he truly needed to change his true self in order to get a pass into society. It took Moussa a while to accept himself and the way in which the system works. When Moussa began making peace with himself and accepting himself just the way he was, that is when the society started smiling him.

He had wanted to blend in so bad, but nothing worked. Then he discovered the emotionally intelligent part of him. He realized the only way for him to be free from these awful treatments he had been receiving was for him to connect with his inner self. Nevertheless, when you also understand the emotions of people around you, you can use them to your own benefit. You can harness those feelings and use them as your shield when the need arises.

Additionally, you will also need a very big chunk of Emotional Intelligence in order to succeed at work or in your professional life. You will need it to relate with others in school. You will also need Emotional Intelligence in your career path in order to be successful. This is how important Emotional Intelligence can be. I bet you can now see the reason why some people want to learn this outstanding trait overnight. The question one should ask him or herself now is if it is possible to exude this outstanding trait in one day.

Imagine waking up one morning with an emotionless feeling? Can you picture yourself in that state? Don't get it twisted; I'm not implying that being expressionless is an awful state to be. In fact, it is an outstanding trait that can only be mastered by the disciplined. But just picture yourself waking up like that without going through any form of training at all, without putting in much effort, and without working towards that goal. Do you think that is possible?

If you are of the thought that such cannot happen overnight, then I would say you are right. If you are also thinking in the direction of believing such a thing can happen in one day, then I won't rule your assertions wrong either. It is important to know that everybody has his or her own limit. Aside from that, there are forces which can push us to be what we don't even expect to be. There are forces that can change us totally from the inside in a single swoop without even recognizing the change at first.

This is what may happen to you when you become emotionally intelligent overnight. First, you must have had or possessed such outstanding trait as we outlined in Chapter Two of this book. You must have been identified with lots of characteristics and traits pointing towards one thing – Emotional Intelligence. For example, you must have been caring towards others, you must have been empathetic towards the emotions of your friends and family, you must have been able to understand your own emotions, and you must have been able to give listening ears and great advice when the need arises. These are just a few of the characters you must have exuded before growing your Emotional Intelligence overnight.

Secondly, you must have been having the notion of becoming a master of your feelings. It is important to know that things just don't happen without our consent or desire for them to happen. For you to develop this outstanding trait overnight, then you must have first desired for it to happen. You must have wished for the power to control your emotions. That would open up a whole new channel in you for the development of this trait. Desiring something means your whole body and mind wants it, thus making sure they are both prepared for the reception of what you desire. That way, you won't have a problem trying to adjust yourself.

When we prepare our mind toward becoming a master of our emotions, we are definitely making sure everything is intact. Desiring the outstanding trait is one thing, but preparing your mind is another different thing entirely. Prepare yourself adequately because Emotional Intelligence can come with a lot of perseverance and patience. Now, the question is, how patient are you? Can you really look the other way in a stressed and tensed situation? If you can't do this, then how do you plan on mastering your emotions? Thus, desire the trait, and then prepare yourself.

Thirdly, you should also learn to know what to do at the right time. This is a very important characteristics only true Stoics and masters of Emotional Intelligence can wield as many times as they like. Knowing how to act in certain circumstances or situations will definitely build you up emotionally in no time. When you comport yourself well even in times of crisis, when you stay calm even during turmoil, when you smile even during disturbances, it's not because you don't have feelings or emotions running through you, but because reacting negatively won't solve anything, and you know this better than anyone.

Instead, you chose to remain calm and collected. You chose to think about damage control instead of going crazy over the whole situation. The funny part of every tensed situation is that when you stay calm and look deep into it, you will realize that the solution and panacea had been right there staring at you. All you needed to do was to think fast and stop allowing your emotions to take the better part of you. This is how confusing emotions can be. This is why many great men of today point at emotions as the number one killer of ideas and dreams.

When you start putting your emotions first, you will achieve very little in life. Believe it or not, putting your emotions first without doing the right thing at the right time will spoil a whole lot of things for you. It will damage the relationships you have toiled to build for years with family and friends. At work, you will have a strained relationship with your co-workers, which can be very bad for you no matter how you interpret that. Things will just stand still in your life with no one ready to connect with you except your ego. Therefore, always do the right thing at the right time.

Fourthly, you should learn to keep the cup of your spirituality flowing no matter what. It is important to know that when others neglect you or turn their back against you totally, only one thing will remain – your inner self. This is the part of you that can never leave you but can definitely neglect you. It all depends on how strong your spirituality levels are.

In case you don't know, our Spirituality level can hasten up the improvement of our Emotional Intelligence and vice versa. If you say both Emotional Intelligence and Spirituality are two sides to a coin, then you are not entirely wrong. No matter what you do, don't allow it to affect your Spirituality because it would always come in handy when the need arises.

And when you have your Spirituality levels intact, then I don't see anything that would stop you in getting your Emotional Intelligence level back up in one night.

Be that as it may, you should try a whole lot of meditation whenever you feel stressed or tensed about a situation. If you feel the situation is going to take a very big chunk of your emotions, then start meditating in your mind. This will help you stay calm and vanish the emotions that had been building up inside of you. All thanks to technology, you can also try out lots of apps which can help you reshuffle your emotions if the need arises.

Additionally, having someone to look up to can also come in handy when the need arises. Trust me; sometimes it can be very hard to maintain the same level of Spirituality over a long period of time all by yourself. This is where you need a spiritual coach, a real-life spiritual mentor, a well-known spiritual leader, or even a spiritual role model. That way, you would have someone to keep you on your toes, someone who's spiritual life is worthy of emulation, someone who will be ready to listen to your woes and drag you back up whenever you fall.

Fifthly, always keep a to-do list, every blessed day of your life. As a beginner, this is the first thing I'm going to tell you if you come to me with the problem of not being able to discover the emotionally intelligent side of you. I would tell you to go back home and make a list of the things you would want to do today and the day after that until infinity. It is very normal for beginners of Emotional Intelligence to slip up and allow their emotions to take control over them in certain situations, especially when they have tried hard to dodge the situation. Some might even forget Emotional Intelligence exists for a while and act on without caution.

This is why I would recommend a to-do list being a novice. Go home, make your list. Point out the crazy scenes from the past and how you reacted to the situation. Then point out areas where you need to brush off and the ones you would need to adjust totally. This is a very good start. After making your list, then see how things go from there. You will be shocked at how well you will respond to any situation that comes knocking.

Now, that is not all. I always make sure I tell those beginners the truth of Emotional Intelligence. It is important to know that even the masters of this trait didn't get it right in one swing. So, there are going to be one or two glitches on your first few days. If at all such things may occur, then write them down also. Learn from them. We are all improving every day. Ripple by ripple, you will also get there. And if your friends and family start noticing any change in you, then you should know that Emotional Intelligence is taking your life to a whole new level.

Sixthly, set your principles and values before starting out. It is important to know that nothing can be achieved in a year, not to mention overnight without setting the foundation; core values and principles. These values and principles would serve as the base of every idea, notion, tenet, character, and so much more. That way, when everything ends up falling apart or going south, the one thing that will remain is your values. They will set the pace for you to follow.

Thus, if you don't have a value or principle that would guide you all through this journey until you become a master yourself, then I would strongly recommend you get one for yourself. How would you find your way back to yourself when your emotions have already taken you over completely? How would you find the right path to follow as regards Emotional Intelligence if you didn't have your values and principles to guide you through it? You can't just wake up one morning with the idea of becoming a master of Emotional Intelligence. Something must have driven the idea out of you. Something must have grown the seeds in you.

Now, that something is your value; don't lose it. Don't get carried away along the line, forgetting the exact thing that brought you here. We all have our own different principles and values which can be very distinct from one another. Don't emulate someone else's. I will never advise you to do that. Form your own values and principles. Look for something that would be important to you, something you can easily uphold. That is the only way you would be able to become emotionally intelligent overnight.

Lastly, always believe in yourself and your abilities. If you don't believe in yourself, no one will. At the end of the day, you are all you have left, thus, better start seeing the potentials in you. Better start seeing the possibilities surrounding you and making good use of them to your own benefit. If you believe you can do it, then nothing should stand in your way of success. All you need to have is a whole lot of determination, commitment, and patience. The rest will be history in no time.

Believe in your abilities and the whole world would see you for what you truly are, and that is someone who is emotionally intelligent. This is the secret recipe no master of Emotional Intelligence would tell you. Many of them would start quoting authors and popular scholars just to make their simple point sound cumbersome. But, if you truly listen attentively to what they have been spewing, then you would realize that believing in oneself is a very important part of mastering your emotions.

Boosting your Emotional Intelligence overnight is very possible. The journey of a thousand miles begins with a bold step, and that bold step is what you need as regards boosting your Emotional Intelligence. If you are ready, determined, and committed, nothing will stop you from achieving your goals. Be that as it may, the next chapter will delve into Emotional Intelligence and relationships. I know this is the chapter you've all been waiting for, so just flip on over.

Chapter Six

7 Tips to Increase Your EQ for Better Relationships

The primary aim of Emotional Intelligence is to be able to maintain and manage better relationships with the people around you. Either at work or at home, in whatsoever situation you find yourself in, the ability to maintain and manage these connections lies with us. Additionally, the way we hold on to a relationship also determines how well we cherish that relationship. For example, the way we would hold the connection between us and our best friends dear is definitely different from the way we hold the connection between us and our co-workers.

A relationship is all that matters in today's world. No matter how you turn it, you will realize that we alone can't live in the state of autarky no matter how hard we try. We can't stay isolated forever. There is always a need for us to interact with one another. Now, this is where Emotional Intelligence comes in. It helps us foster our relationship with friends and family with an understanding of our emotions. It believes that if you can truly keep your emotions in check, then there is no limit to the things you would achieve and conquer in the world today.

As a matter of fact, Emotional Intelligence is not just referring to or preaching the management and control of one's emotion alone, it cut across the management and influence of the emotions of others too. If we can achieve this feat, then managing relationships and connections shouldn't be hard to pull off. In an organizational atmosphere where 60% of the workers are male and 40% of the workers are female, a test was carried out on the level of the workers' Emotional Intelligence and the result was highly predictable.

Almost every male in the organization got above 70% of the score, with the females failing woefully to a very large extent (please note that this is not in any way a direct or indirect jibe to the feminist). According to the Emotional Intelligence experts, they believed the result of the test was highly correct due to the fact that women often fail to separate their emotions from anything they do, including their professional career.

A career woman today with everything going on for her would still feel emotional towards something. It's the natural order of things with women. They are naturally bound to think toward emotion. But with Emotional Intelligence, things can be different this time. They can have a balance between themselves as regards being emotional, thereby, making them become masters of their emotions.

When we react to certain issues in our relationships, we tend to go overboard with things. For example, in order to get the much-needed attention that we seek, we try to build mountains out of nothing. In the end, we might get the attention we had craved, but at a very costly price. Our relationship can end up getting strained or even severed at most. And if at all we are still lucky to have the relationship, then our connection would definitely get weak.

When you see two people growing all over each other, then you should assume they just got lucky to have found each other. As a matter of fact, both of them must have passed through challenging phases in the course of their relationship but still maintained patience and perseverance. There are occasions where only one person in the relationship is the mature one. There are cases where the man or the woman might be an emotionally intelligent fellow. Now, that is what it takes for a relationship to be as strong as ever. If you want your relationships with people to stand the test of time, then you really need to understand how they operate.

You need to know when their off moments are, you need to know what drives them crazy, and you need to know what they feel at all times. That is the only way you would be abreast with the happenings in their life and the best way to do this is to learn to read their emotions correctly. We would then be able to help them out when the need arises. We would be able to tend to them whenever they feel down. We would be able to know what they want at the right time. We would also be able to predict their next move even without them telling us. If we are a very good master of emotions, we would make new relationship more easily than we lose them.

I once dated a very immature lady and I must confess that the relationship was really hectic. As a master of Emotional Intelligence, I made sure I overlooked her shortcomings and mistakes because of the likeness I had had for her. Thus, I became the mature one in the relationship. Along the line, she started complaining that I was too expressionless. According to her, she didn't even know my emotions anymore. Sometimes, she would want to irritate me by force, but being a master of my own emotions, I had always managed to stay clear of trouble.

I was able to manipulate and sway our relationship through the hurdles of life. But it got to a point where I just got tired of being the mature one. Emotional Intelligence might guide me via that journey but my will, patience, and commitment kept my sanity. You need to have a mixture of all these key ingredients in order to have a successful relationship with another person. Emotional Intelligence may help you open up pathways for a successful relationship, but if the other person is also not willing to adjust or control their own emotions, then your effort might just seem fruitless.

Many great relationships today are built on the ability to checkmate our emotions. When both of us are masters of our own emotions, there is no rock our relationship won't surpass. No matter how stiff the obstacles may be, we will always sail pass it. Now, what will this chapter do? This particular chapter will help you see possible ways in which you can improve your relationship. It will help you see how you can save your relationship from dying off. And it will also show you ways to which you can reconnect with your friends and family in cases of lost connection.

1. **Avoid Negative Thoughts and Emotions:** The only possible way you can see potential and goodness in your relationships with other people is by always focusing on the brighter side. When you always immerse yourself in the possibilities surrounding your relationships, then your relationships will thrive. Now, how do you go about this? It's simple. Just try and erase any negative thoughts in your mind towards your relationships. When you do that, there will be little or no problems at all. And if these problems arise, you will be filled with more than enough zeal to tackle them.

Pushing back negative thoughts and emotions about our relationships can be quite difficult. For example, losing the trust you share with a person can end up spoiling the relationship. We all know that trust is the foundation of every relationship. Without this trust, there can really be no connection between us and others. You can imagine building a relationship with someone you don't trust. That will just end up being disastrous.

A good relationship thrives on good emotions and thoughts. If at all times, all you guys think are good thoughts about one another, there would certainly be no issue at all. Although this is easier said than done, you can at least give it a shot. I know these negative emotions and thoughts will surely cross your path, but the way and manner in which you handle yourself during these events will determine how far the relationship will go.

Janice and Wayne were good friends in the university. Their meeting was as a result of a strange circumstance which led to their unbreakable bond and connection over the past two years. One can boldly say that they are each other's best friend. However, Janice saw Wayne smoking weed and she as a person has an irritation for the plant, let alone the users of it. Instead of telling Wayne how she felt immediately as Emotional Intelligence would have strongly supported, she kept it to herself.

Now, their connection began getting weaker by the day because of the negative thoughts and emotions Janice had gathered and accumulated in her mind about Wayne. It is important to note that being honest with others is an important attribute of Emotional Intelligence. Yet, Janice wasn't. She kept her thoughts and opinions to herself, thereby, feeding herself with nothing but negative emotions and thoughts. These same emotions would be the tool for breaking the bond between them.

If Janice had been honest with Wayne, if Janice had called Wayne to the table and emptied her guts, and if Janice had voiced out, their relationship of two years wouldn't have hit the rocks. You never can tell if that was Wayne's first time smoking pot. You never can tell if he was being cajoled, bullied or brainwashed by the other kids into smoking with them. But instead, Janice jumped to a conclusion - a conclusion that ended their relationship for good.

Be that as it may, we should always learn to look at the situation very closely before jumping to conclusions. We should always be sure we have our facts before allowing our thoughts and emotions to grow negatively. If at all our emotions end up taking the better side of us, then we should not forget to be honest with our partners. At least they deserve that from us. Always see the brighter side of things no matter how shrewd they might look. That is the only way we can be sure that we aren't making a mistake.

2. Listen More, Choose Your Words Carefully, and be a Good Communicator: Have you ever seen a working relationship where dialogue wasn't practiced more than usual? Many people forget that this tool works wonders in a relationship, especially in times of crisis and turmoil. When everything seems to be going south in your relationships, the best way to get things back on track is to be a good communicator. And what does a good communicator do? He listens attentively and speaks perfectly when the need arises.

Believe it or not, dialogue is the best way to foster your relationships. With the mixture of both dialogue and Emotional Intelligence, there would be nothing stopping you from establishing any form of connection in your relationships. Even in your place of work, you should always endeavor to be a good communicator amidst your fellow employees or employers. That way, you will be given the much-needed respect you deserve and the working relationships will improve rapidly.

As an emotionally intelligent person, what you should always be working toward is to become a better version of who you were yesterday. When you meet new people, your words should clarify how different you are from the rest. When you talk, you should be mindful of the emotions of others. Don't say things that will hurt them in any way, no matter crazy your emotions might be. The focus of Emotional Intelligence is to keep your emotions in check anyway. Be sure to do a good job.

What if you had a bad day? How would you manage your emotions afterward? Emotionally intelligent people always proffer solution to their emotional problems and to that of the people around them. If ever you find yourself being stuck at a particular point, then don't feel bad at all. Instead, look for a way around the solution. Additionally, when you are relating to others around you, you should learn to be a good listener. The floor isn't meant for you alone. Let others have a say, too. That is the only way your relationships will flourish.

3. Be Empathetic at all Times: What more do you need to know about Emotional Intelligence if not being empathetic toward everyone around you? The ability to know what others are feeling is a rare gift mastered by only emotionally intelligent people in the world. If you possess this gift, then kudos to you. Look for clues and pointers in you aren't very close to the person but still, care about him or her. Stay calm and collected each time you are around that person. That is the only way you will be able to know what their true emotions are.

Some people are very good at masking their emotions from others. No matter how hard you try to take a peep into their inner self, they just won't budge. Nonetheless, you still need to be emotionally attentive to such people. You need to show them genuine love and care. That is the only language they understand. This is because these set of people find it very hard to trust people. Thus, you need to earn trust. Soothe them with your words of encouragement and support. Show them what life will be like if only they can trust and open up their inner feelings.

Empathy in the professional sense has also been a driving force in today's world. It is believed that many top companies in the country today now focus on the Emotional Intelligence levels of their employees. They believe if one is filled with empathy, then there would certainly be a good working relationship between the employee and their clients. In other words, it would mean additional revenue for these companies. If these employees can continue to keep their clients happy, then it's a good thing for the company.

Sometimes, before we truly understand the emotions running through some people, we need to actually place ourselves in their position. We would need to first sit back and watch how everything played out from their angle. If we keep looking at things from our own angle, then we are bound to always misunderstand the emotions of others, and that negates the principle of empathy.

4.   Know Your Push Buttons: I would strongly advise you to keep your push buttons far from where others might see them. In fact, bury them deep if you can. That is the only way you won't get stressed or even tensed over little things. You really need to make sure you are familiar with your breaking points. Always make sure you are in control of them. And if you can't control them, then at least be sure to always be conscious of them. That way, you will be able to apply the much needed precautionary measures when the need arises.

If weed turns you off completely, they always make sure you ring it out to the ears of everyone around you. That way, they will be able to avoid using it around you. If drinking is what irritates you, then make sure your circle is clean and sober. You need to set boundaries for yourself in order to have prosperous and fruitful relationships with the people around you. And if you feel you can make compromises, feel free to do so.

Thus, let us know our weak points for a better relationship. If you are dating someone who knows all your push buttons, then that person would know exactly what to avoid so as not to get you filled with negative emotions. Well, except in cases where that person might start pushing those buttons intentionally. But as an emotionally intelligent person, you should be able to tell the difference. Whichever way it is, always make sure you have a precautionary measure to your push buttons.

5.   Approach Adversities Maturely: One important thing that accompanies all relationships is ups and downs. There will definitely be good times and bad times. But remember, when the good times come, don't get too carried away. Instead, prepare for the bad. I'm not saying you shouldn't enjoy the good time while it lasts. As a matter of fact, I would advise you to enjoy every bit of it - but not without preparing yourself for the bad that may follow.

When the time comes for the bad moments, your preparation will now come in handy. You will now be able to bounce back from the tribulations like it's nothing. When I mean preparation, I'm referring to mental and emotional preparation. Now that is where Emotional Intelligence comes in. Emotional Intelligence will equip you emotionally and mentally to withstand any obstacles and adversities you might face.

Instead of reacting weakly, wrongly, and emotionally, we will be able to react maturely and properly. Instead of gathering negative emotions and thoughts in our hearts, we will be able to focus on the possibilities around us. We will be able to think positive. Thus, always keep the optimism, even when things aren't looking good in your relationship. The way you approach your problems is definitely the way you would address them.

6.   Reflect: Always reflect on the events and situations that have happened in your relationships over the past years. Reflections are signs of overcoming our troubles and obstacles. Reflection comes after overcoming the trials that may have made our relationships unbearable. It is important to know that reflections do not make us weak, nor do they make us vulnerable, instead they make us even more mature and wise.

Only great men reflect back to their previous actions. That way, they will be able to pick up corrections in case of future reoccurrence. Along the line of reflecting on our relationships, we would realize the strengths and weaknesses of our actions. We would be able to replay our actions again and again until we learn from them. If you are dating a temperamental person who loses his or her cool at the slightest provocation, the best way for you to approach such a person is to stay calm and understand their emotions.

Afterward, you can take your time to reflect on the events that left you puzzled. Make sure you weigh your strengths and weaknesses during your moment of reflection. Think deep about what started the misunderstanding in the first place. Do not cultivate the habit of playing the blame game. Instead, know where your faults lie and work on them. Reflections are created for just one reason, and that is to be a better version of what you are now. Reflect well and make good use of them.

7. Admit and Accept Your Fault when you are Wrong: It is important to know that accepting one's faults doesn't make you smaller or inferior. Instead, it will make you a person with a big heart. When we know our faults, the best thing to do is to admit to them and make amends immediately before it gets out of hand. Thanks to Emotional Intelligence, accepting our faults and knowing where our mistakes lie brings us closer to our friends and family. We will even become closer, with ours bond getting stronger by the day.

Many believe that relationships are meant to be made and broken. Well, that is just not true. Relationships are indeed meant to be kept and improved upon. Are you having issues maintaining your relationships on a professional or personal level? Then have you tried Emotional Intelligence? If no, then this chapter is written just for you. Give Emotional Intelligence a shot in your relationships this time, and you will be shocked at how amazing things would flow.

Chapter Seven

19 Ways to Improve Your Emotions in 2019

2019 is a year filled with new, exciting adventures, as well as challenges. It is a year which further exposes the 21st century as the age of technological revolutions, medical breakthroughs, scientific innovations, and so much more. Now, let's take a very long jump from all these great and abstract feats. How about relationships? How has 2019 become the new age for a modernized and sophisticated form of relationships? How has 2019 fashioned the connection of one person to another? Has it really made a reasonable impact in this direction?

Without mincing many words, it won't be far from the truth if we say 2019 has also contributed its own quota to the developing of relationships and connections within the world. People now see relationships, connections, and Spirituality in a whole new light. Instead of the traditional methods of growing and maintaining relationships, there have been a whole lot of improved tips and techniques which have proven to be far more effective and efficient. Now, this is where Emotional Intelligence comes into play.

As a brand new idea that was conceived over a decade by a popular scholar, Emotional Intelligence has thrived over the years with lots of people adopting this idea and building upon the foundation. As an advocate of emotional control, Emotional Intelligence goes deeper than you can imagine. It touches other aspects like Spirituality, connections, relationships, motivation, success, and so much more. According to the tenets, if we can truly control our emotions, if we can truly keep our feelings in check, and if truly we can understand our feelings as well as the feelings of others, then there is no limit to what we will achieve.

Be that as it may, 2019 comes with its own distractions and complications, too. It is as if the more it becomes glamorous, the more it becomes even more distracting. The world today is filled with lots of these side attractions that may sway you off the path to becoming a master of your own emotions. For example, there are now a whole lot of trigger points which would make you lose focus or concentration even without knowing it. Thanks to globalization, the world today has now contracted into one whole bunch.

New inventions, ideas, and innovations might not really go down well with you, thereby making you lose yourself in the process. I can still recall vividly when the current United States of America's president, in the person of Donald Trump, won the election by defeating Hilary Clinton to emerge victoriously. My opposite neighbor, who had always carried himself well, lost his calm that same moment right in my presence. I must say, I'd never seen a man get so stressed, tensed, angry, and frustrated all at the same time.

He swore and cursed for almost an hour before he could get a grip of himself. I totally understood his frustration, probably because he is Mexican and was highly concerned about Donald Trump's policies that negate the growth of his race in the United States. Now, this reaction from someone who had always comported himself well got me thinking. Was 2019 really that different? Or had we all evolved to a point where Emotional Intelligence hardly works?

It didn't take me long to figure the whole thing out. 2019 comes with its own complications indeed, and the frustrations we get from these complications are mostly stored up inside of us, causing stress and anxiety. When the slightest thing around us starts irritating us, then we really need to go back into our spiritual realm. That way, we will be able to reconnect with ourselves, thereby, going to our principles and values which have marked our true self from the beginning. If we are losing touch with our Emotional Intelligence, then we need to prepare our minds and focus on the possibilities around us.

We need to regain the consciousness that once held our emotions. We need to really understand the basis that defines our emotional breakdown or meltdown. That way, we would be able to know what our emotions are and what they really entail. Sometimes, we get so worked up due to the pressures we might have faced at work. Some of us work three to four shift, just to make hands meet, thus, there would be very little or no tolerance at all on our part. Additionally, a simple coffee expresso machine or toaster might go bad without our knowledge, thus, dashing our hope for an early morning coffee.

This disappointment might not go down well with us, thus, making us lose our cool. Little things like that seldom have a way of making us lose our self in the process. When this happens, keeping calm is the best way to go about it. This is what every master of Emotional Intelligence will tell you to do. Remember, we can't control how we feel, but we can definitely control the outcome of those feelings. Now, it is your choice to either go berserk or act maturely. But trust me, the latter would be preferable.

It is understandable if you lose your cool over that espresso machine, especially if you are a low-income earner. There are lots of thoughts that would definitely go through your head. You would start imagining how to go about fixing it or getting a new one if it's old and worn out. Nonetheless, using your Emotional Intelligence to tackle the situation would be a lot better.

Now, what will this chapter do? This chapter will familiarize you with the face of Emotional Intelligence and how to improve on it in the year 2019. There are lots of ways in which Emotional Intelligence can be improved this year, especially judging from the present face of things. Losing your cool and giving in to your emotions is quite easy with the present state of the world today, so how do we really improve our Emotional Intelligence in 2019?

1. **Keep Everything Normal:** When we tend to keep our tempos up, there is every tendency that we might lose our emotions. Always try to stay calm whenever you feel uncomfortable. That way, your temperature would go down. Additionally, you can also give in to more sleep. When we retire

early, we tend to get ourselves refreshed. Our mental and physical health would improve beyond recognition.

Additionally, we would also recommend you to keep your room at a normal temperature. Make sure everything is set for you to have a sound sleep. Sometimes, we tend to get stressed with the harsh weather conditions. We are likely to get more tensed in a very hot atmosphere. Thus, keep the atmosphere normal as it would help you become a better version of what you were yesterday.

2. Be Bold to Try out New Things: Be bold enough to test new waters. Don't just confine yourself to a particular spot or position. Challenge yourself to try out new boundaries. Thank God 2019 brings out new things around us; make sure you use them well. Be sure to look for new adventures. Be sure to test yourself beyond your areas of specialization. If your emotions are just a little beyond control, then I would recommend you know what drives it crazy and what keeps it in control.

That is the only way you would improve. Know your boundaries first, and then start working toward progressing with them. Start working towards moving past the boundaries of your emotions. In other words, try out new things. Try out new hobbies. Go out and make new friends. Make sure you meet new people. Engage yourself in your new activities. If this happens, there are certain ways in which trying out new things would serve as a stress reliever.

When you try out new things, you will be immersed with the mysteries surrounding them. These mysteries that surround them will be the mechanism that will push you into becoming more confident with your emotions.

3. Create New Circles: 2019 is a year of plush and plenty. It is a year filled with life and prosperity. Thus, why not be among those that would explore this exciting and amazing year? Make new friends, meet new people, and create new circles or group. For example, if you are a regular member of a certain mental health social group, how about trying out new exciting groups, too? How about exploring what the other groups have to offer?

Now, always put it at the back of your mind that people will always want to interact with you even if you push them away. In this modern world, some people just don't take no for an answer. You might be shocked to discover that it is these same people that are most amazing to connect with. Connecting with them would give you no problem at all. Notwithstanding, improve your Emotional Intelligence by increasing your social circle.

In case you don't know, having a lot of friends and family to connect with would kill off any spirit of loneliness in you. Interacting and sharing ideas with your friends and family would help make you feel great in the end. When you have someone to talk to, someone to relate with, and someone to connect with, you will come to find life very easy - trust me.

4. Paint or Color if You Feel Stressed: This is one method that works all the time. A lot of people believe doing what you love at your moment of stress will help drop the stress tempos and levels. This is very true. Additionally, what you love doing in the time of stress and loneliness is quite different from what others love doing. Coincidentally, if taking a walk or listening to music is your thing, then there is a chance that this same walk or music can be a thing for several people too.

But one thing that works well is painting and coloring. First, it helps you get back to normal. It brings your levels down whenever they are too high, thereby, making you feel amazing in the end. Additionally, painting your fears and worries away can also be in the form of a new type of art. You get to make yourself feel alright and you also get to add the painting to your collection. Now, that is a win-win situation.

Whenever you feel tense, stressed, and want to build on your Emotional Intelligence, painting and coloring is one way out of it. Your stress levels would determine the colors you pick. And one way or the other, your mind would just seem to contract back to normal. If ever you feel uncomfortable or angry over a certain decision or mistake you've made, then I strongly recommend you go into painting. Pour your frustration into it and you will come out as good as new.

5. Become Incommunicado if the Need Arises: There are times in life when we just want to be alone, no matter how hard we try to stay focused and relate with the people around us. We just seldom feel disconnected with these loads of people around us, who are probably trying hard to make us feel better or even get our attention. Seriously, it's not all about the connection we feel for one another. Sometimes, the best way to become the best version of ourselves is by staying disconnected from all things.

That is the only way we will be able to move forward. That is the only way we would be able to realize what the problem really is. Sometimes, all we need is time alone to refresh ourselves. Feel free to stay off the radar for a while. It's part of the process of becoming a better version of yourself. Now, in this computerized and technologically advanced world, how can one stay off the grid? It's pretty simple.

Start by going to a secluded area and stay in solitude. Stay clear off your phones and gadgets. In fact, stay clear off any form of notification devices that may enable others to reach you. The amount of time you stay in solitude is mostly determined by how much time you need to get yourself back to normal. And remember, all you need is just a little bit of peace and quiet. The rest will work itself out naturally.

6. Eat Good Food and Diet if You Can: There is a certain food that would enable you to react in a certain way or even improve and decrease our level of Emotional Intelligence as time progresses. When you eat something you shouldn't have, there is every tendency that the food you have taken in will do some damage in you. For example, taking in much sugar would cause quite a lot of damage to your system, even though you still need sugar.

Also, there are some foods we would strongly recommend for you if at all you are trying to work on your Emotional Intelligence. How about adding Omega-3 Fatty Acids in your daily diet? Trust me; they are very good for your Emotional Intelligence levels. They will help maintain your levels as well as increase your interactive rate with the people around you.

So, what kind of food should we consume? Obviously, food that contains this particular acid would be more advisable. For example, salmon, flaxseed, walnuts, and other oil supplements are just perfect for you. In as much as they help the body in making sure the depression rate is at the minimal, they also help in giving the body a whole lot of other nutrients that will come in handy. Eat what you must, but always think Omega-3 Fatty Acids first.

7. Exercise and Aerobics Would Help, Too: I haven't seen a book or heard someone that had made an important criticism or complaint against exercising the body. With a whole lot of books stressing the benefits that come with exercising the body, even a dumb person knows how effective and efficient exercise can be in our lives. Wither you are taking a mere walk or doing a rigorous workout in the nearby gym, it's all to the realization of one thing – a perfect body.

Now, how does exercise relate to improved Emotional Intelligence? I'll tell you. When you exercise the body, your body attracts healthiness in return. In other words, our body ensures that every possible system in it functions properly. Additionally, exercising the body helps keep the body circulation rate normal and when the circulation rate becomes normal, our mood becomes better. Aside from that, you would also be taking good care of yourself.

Exercise works wonders in our body in more ways than you can imagine. It stretches out the muscles and joints, it relaxes the body, and it ensures the body is in a good working condition. When you exercise your body, it will make you look fit. In other words, give you a dream body, thus giving you the confidence to be who you want to be around your friends and family. That way, you will definitely be motivated, inspired, and feel amazing.

8. Clear Your Head with Walks and Strolls: Always cultivate the habit of going out for a walk or stroll. You can either do this alone or with friends and family if you want to. Instead of staying bottled up inside your apartment in solitude, you can also go out there and embrace the world. Taking a walk around the park, strolling the neighborhood, or even jogging to the fields would help you clear your head. It would help you reduce tension and stress.

Are you angry about a particular event or situation? Then walk it over. Are you mad about something you did and weren't really proud of? Then stroll over it. Walking around or just taking a stroll would help relieve the stress you are feeling. It would kill off any feelings of loneliness. And trust me; there is a good chance of you meeting someone new. There is a big possibility of you connecting with someone.

Meanwhile, ensure these walks and strolls are in your schedule, so as not to inconvenience yourself in the end. Go out there and enjoy nature. Take a walk to the park or woods and see nature firsthand. You would be surprised at how amazing you would feel before heading back home. Be that as it may, walking solves your problem of fatigue, reduces depression to the minimum, and boosts your level of Emotional Intelligence.

9. Never Let That Smile Leave Your Face: Your smile is your selling point. It is your most enticing weapon, which you can use anytime you feel uncomfortable, stressed, or even lost. When things start getting out of control, then you should start thinking of flashing that set of teeth out for people to see. Smiling is a gesture that keeps us out of trouble. Even in the most tensed situation of our lives, a single smile would make everything become normal.

Now, wouldn't you rather smile than go through a whole lot of hurt? Wouldn't you rather smile to avoid those erupting emotions in you from damaging the good relationships you had toiled to keep? Even when we don't feel too good about a certain decision concerning us, we shouldn't show our outburst in an inconveniencing way. If we know we can't contain the emotions or turn the situation to our own benefit, then we should just smile over it.

A smile would reassure the other partner in a relationship that all is well. A smile would rekindle the connection that might have seemed to be lost. With just a smile, you can melt even the hardest of hearts. We can get through to even those that aren't ready to open up if only we just smile at every possible situation. That would only make our mood even better. A beautiful smile will make sure our mind stays calm and our heart rate normal.

10. Learn about Postures and Explore to the Best of Your Ability: Emotional Intelligence comes with staying confident and being confident comes with carrying yourself well in an amazing way. This is where having a good posture comes into play. Make 2019 your year of good living. Make 2019 your year of great confidence and power. It is important to know that when we tend to act smart around the people we care about, our relationships will definitely thrive.

But when we start acting sluggishly, when we start acting dull and emotional, the relationship will suffer. Thus, sit properly at all times. Stand properly also. If you are walking, then walk properly, too. That is the only way you will be able to exude confidence which will lead to motivation, inspiration, and success. When you carry yourself with so much grace, people would want to really relate with you even more.

11. Don't Joke with the Power of Vitamin D: Allow Vitamin D be your best friend. Always make sure you get it in surplus so as to be able to hold your body and soul together. Immerse yourself in the power of the smiling sun. Afterward, watch yourself grow and remain ravishing. If we keep looking fresh and amazing, then there is no telling how much we will achieve in the year 2019.

When you take at least 15 minutes of your time to take in the brightness of the sun, your mood will definitely improve and your Emotional Intelligence will become just as sharp as that of any master. Remember, when the body is in good working conditions, nothing will be able to stop you from reaching the peak of your world.

12.   Plan a Retreat Sometime: Your body needs every bit of relaxation you can give it. Sometimes, all we need to do is to go down a little in order to come out even stronger. Are you feeling tensed at work lately? Do you feel stuffed at home with everything happening around you always getting the better side of you? Do you feel you are reaching a point in life where you just won't be able to take it anymore? Then plan a getaway.

You can plan a getaway with family, friends or even alone. This would definitely lift up your spirits and keep you motivated. You can also go on a spiritual journey. This would make you realize what truly lies ahead of you. Make sure you set this example in the year 2019. As a matter of fact, make it occasional. Find a place where you will always love to be and make sure you spend some time there, if not frequently, at least occasionally.

You would be surprised at how your emotions would drop to normal. A getaway would ease your mind as it will bring in relaxation. Trust me - depression would be very far away from your doorstep. Walk away temporarily from the troubles and crises in your life and things will definitely set out fine for you.

13.   Always be Grateful: According to a wise saying, scaling gratitude will definitely lead to a higher altitude. A mind that is filled with gratitude would definitely receive nothing but joy and happiness in return. Thus, learn to cultivate this attitude within yourself. No matter how little anything might be, so long it affects your life positively, show gratitude. Be thankful always for what you have, what you have become, and what you will be.

A mind that is filled with gratitude would know no greed, pain, and ego. It would be a mind filled with satisfaction, love, and joy. Now, that kind of mind is what you truly need in order to develop your Emotional Intelligence even further. In order to reassemble and reconnect with your inner self even better, you would need to have a mind devoid of ungratefulness, greed, and ingratitude.

Thus, I would recommend you take this seriously. Every day of your life, before you lay your back on the bed, make sure you reflect on the things that had happened to you all through that 24 hour timeline. Then think of the things you need to be thankful for. That way, your mind will be full of positivity, thereby, making your outlook also change for the better. A thankful soul is a blessed mind; never forget that.

14. Keep Records of Things by Writing Your Experiences Down: Whether you decide to keep a journal or a diary, just try and have something you can use to write your vital experiences down. There is always a great relief that comes with this journal keeping. Writing can be a way of keeping yourself abreast of the happenings in your life. It can also be a way of releasing the tensions and stress that have built up in you already.

A lot of masters of Emotional Intelligence would tell you this is a good way to bring your levels down. For example, if you have something bothering you at work or at home, then the best way to make yourself fell alright about it is to write it down somewhere. That way, you would be able to think of a way in which you can face them squarely. These tactics should be employed in 2019 if truly you want to improve your Emotional intelligence.

15. Feel Free to say NO When the Need Arises: This is the number one killer of every relationship out there. Because we might have a certain level of connection with our friends and family, we would now be obligated to make them feel special by any means necessary, even though it means inconveniencing ourselves in the end. This attitude of ours would definitely put us in trouble whether we like it or not.

We can't do everything all by ourselves. We can't go on making ourselves unhappy just because we want to please others. In the end, we will be losing ourselves without us even knowing. We should learn to stop cultivating this habit in the year 2019. Don't hesitate to say no whenever you feel unhappy, pressured, and tensed about a certain situation.

Stop making promises that would put you in trouble in the end. Let this year make a difference in your life. Before making a crucial decision that would make your life unbearable or might not benefit you in the long run, think deeply about it. And if you think you can't handle it, then kindly say NO. No one would hold a gun to your neck when this happens. Don't inconvenience yourself in order to please others. That will be emotionally unintelligent.

16.   Eat a Well-Balanced Diet at all Times: Eating junk or fast foods can be quite disadvantageous to our bodies in the long run. Thus, we should always make sure we eat well in order to maintain a great body. When the body is in a good working condition, we will be able to react well to the happenings in our lives. I have seen people who get easily emotional due to an illness in their body.

Any time my father gets sick, we all know better than to act normal around him. During this phase, he gets easily paranoid and highly emotional at the same time. Thus, we always try to act extra carefully and extra cautious each time we are around him during this phase. As a bus driver, my dad had been accustomed to eating junk. Every morning, he would get a cheeseburger on his way to the bus park, skip the afternoon meal, and mostly eat all forms of pasta for dinner.

Always eat well no matter the schedule of your work and engagements. When you eat well, your body will respond well, there will be a smooth circulation running through you, and every other part will function perfectly well. Both your physical and mental health will be in great shape. Make sure your meals contain the six classes of food. That is one of the ways to stay in great shape.

17. Start with Smaller Goals before Advancing to Bigger Ones: Before the start of 2019, I'm sure you already had your New Year goals and objectives well mapped out. Now, take a good look at them. Do they include achieving bigger things? For example, do you plan on focusing more on the outside than the inside? Do you plan on making a lot of people smile out there? Does it include reconnecting with all lost connections?

If it does, then it's a good thing. But allow me to ask you some questions. Don't you feel those goals are too high for now? Don't you feel you need to really understand yourself and emotions first before understanding someone else's? Making people happy is cool, but have you made yourself happy? This is what I would want you to do, set your goals from this basis. Then build on them until you reach the peak of to your goals.

Start from scratch. You can only make an impact in the lives of others if you make an impact on yours. You can only understand people's emotions and be able to influence them for the better after you have mastered your own emotions. This is how Emotional Intelligence really works. Do this and you will be shocked at how much growth you will achieve all on your own.

Additionally, taking time to reflect on the things we had missed out last year wouldn't be a bad idea. After all, Emotional Intelligence is all about making the best out of your emotions by reflecting on them. In 2019, make sure you don't repeat the same mistakes. Make sure you program yourself into going for only goals that can be realistic and not the ones that are out of your reach. If we focus on what we can't achieve, it brings depression and failure into our lives. And if you feel the goals are important, feel free to break them into parts. That would make them easy to achieve.

18. Know Your Mental State: There is only one way in which we can stay abreast with our mental state and that is by getting ourselves educated about mental issues. If we are aware of our mental issues, we will surely know the stages at which our emotions can be or are currently in. When we know about our mental issues, we will be able to adopt a new way, if possible coin our own methods in bringing down our mental levels back to normal when the need arises.

Having an idea of mental issues will put us ahead of our own emotions. We will be able to tell when and how we feel at a particular time. That way, we would be able to navigate our way through depression, emotional trauma, stress, and so much more. However, if you feel what you are going through is far more than what the little knowledge you know can handle, then feel free to try even more sophisticated means.

19. Always Engage Yourself in Something You Love Doing: Never stop doing what you love, especially if it leaves a smile on your face each time. Whenever you feel down, you should be able to calm yourself with that thing that you love doing. If it is shopping that makes you lively, then go for it so long you have the means to. If it is music that brings the better part of you out into the world, then go into it fully. Don't allow anything stop you from doing what you love doing this year.

When we probably excel at something, then it means we are good at it. Now, that thing, be it yoga, swimming, dancing, and so on, can become a part of us. For example, whenever you feel tensed and you know whistling is the only way to make you feel better, then feel free to whistle. However, you wouldn't want to start whistling loud in your place of work. Just don't stop doing what brings life into you. Continue making yourself happy. That way, your Emotional Intelligence will definitely improve.

So far, 2019 has been a noisy and busy year with lots of events, situations, and activities going on around the globe. If the same thing applies to your own personal life, then I would suggest you find ways to improve yourself and your Emotional Intelligence this year in order to be able to contain yourself and the people around you. Pay close attention to this chapter and make sure you immerse yourself to the 19 special tips we outlined on improving your Emotional Intelligence.

Chapter Eight

The Little-Known Time-Tested Principles to Follow If You Want to Persuade Others

The power of persuasion is an outstanding trait you would only find in 1 out of 20. When one possesses this power, then one is said to have mastered emotions completely. Aside from self-awareness, which deals with identifying your emotions and knowing that they exist, self-control comes next which also deals with understanding your emotions in order to keep your relationships intact. When you have the ability to control the outcome of your own emotions, then everything will definitely fall in line for you.

Empathy comes next. Ripple by ripple, we would now start developing particular care and feeling toward the people around us. What is the use of understanding our own emotions without understanding the emotions of others? When we understand them, our relationships will definitely progress. We will know how they feel at any particular moment even before they start telling us what the problem is. We would be able to approach anybody that comes our way the right way no matter how shrewd the situation may be. We would be able to know when to shoot our shots and when to stay in our shell.

Finally, social skills are the last phase to it and that deals with the power of persuasion. In other words, you have an influence in the life of people around us. Emotional Intelligence would definitely help show you how to exert an influence in the life of others when the need arises. Darlington is a top chef at a prestigious restaurant in town. Though he was the assistant chief chef, people really preferred him to any other person in the restaurant. When Darlington takes orders, he has the ability to influence the customer's decisions for the better.

Darlington would make sure he gets you the best of what you want. It's like he knows his customers' taste buds even before they enter. Thus, when he left the restaurant to open his own makeshift food truck, 80% of the customers left with him. As a matter of fact, Darlington is now an underdog with lots of investors ready to take a chance on him. Now, that is the power of persuasion via Emotional Intelligence, when we have the ability to help people see the possibilities around them. When we have the ability to help others realize what they have been missing which is just right in front of them the whole time, then we can boldly hit our chest to have possessed the power of persuasion.

The power of persuasion comes with being influential. When you are always geared toward making the life of the people around you improve for the better, you are definitely making an impact that would leave you to be more influential than before. It takes just a little bit of sweet talk and a very large amount of Emotional Intelligence for one to be able to influence others. The power of persuasion lies with great men and women, men and women of valor and honor, men and women that have the ability to understand the emotions of the people around them and turn them to their own advantage.

In your relationships, if you hold this power, then I would suggest you wield it appropriately. Some people can be very cunning and greedy. They can also misuse this power in order to achieve their own selfish desires. For example, one man that has greatly misused this power in the course of history is Adolf Hitler himself. This man was popularly known to have possessed true power of persuasion when he rose from nothing to the top of the ranks in Germany. Thanks to his persuasion skills, he was able to influence the whole country into doing his bidding.

Now, what will this chapter do? This chapter will help sensitize you with the different persuasion principles out there. It will help you see persuasion for what it really is and how to further improve on it by following the well-tested principles, philosophical theories, and so much more. Be that as it may, when we look at the people around us closely, we will be able to predict who they are and what they want. We will be able to predict what they are really made of. It is important to know that everyone is configured separately, thus for us to really understand how their emotions would be toward certain situations, we would really need to first understand how they are wired.

I believe this is where we ask those questions that have been disturbing our minds over the years, yeah? We now begin to ask how some people we know can become so persuasive. How can some people be so good at it? Is being emotionally intelligent their topmost secret? How do we go about it? Would I be able to master the power of persuasion within the shortest possible time?

There are lots of techniques and principles one can use in mastering the power of persuasion. These techniques and principles have also being used one way or the other by today's world leaders, be it religious, political, social, business, and so much more. The power of persuasion is a rare gift that will take you places if harnessed properly. It will help you build your relationship from scratch if applied appropriately. And it will help you attain the heights you have always craved for.

I will categorically share these principles into different segments so as to allow you to become familiar with the skills and tactics. First, I would explain the Basics, then move on to General Rule, and finally the Personal Inborn Skills.

The Basics

1. Wrong Assumptions: This is one problem and misconception that has tarnished the image of the power of persuasion. A lot of people believed this act has to do with brainwashing and manipulation. This assumption is very wrong. When you influence the decisions of others positively, then you are simply being persuasive. You are making the person see things in another dimension without sugarcoating your words with lies and falsehood.

Unlike manipulation and brainwashing, where you would have to be cunning and deceitful, being persuasive is a very clean source of being influential. Where manipulation and brainwashing come with the use of force, with making one do what he or she doesn't want to do, and with hurting someone into doing your bidding, persuasion simply deals with the art of making people see pass their short-sightedness. You would make them see the light.

2. No One is Unpersuadable: No matter how shrewd you might think you are, there is still a part of you that can be persuaded, whether you like it or not. All that is needed is to reach that inner part of you that is still soft. Thus, no one is free from the claws of persuasion. It all depends on the way the person approaches you, the timing in which the person might approach you and the situation at hand.

The power of persuasion works on a long term process. First, you need to gain the trust of the people you would want to influence and this might take a very long time. For example, during elections, politicians would want to build a lasting relationship with the electorates as they decide the winners of every election. If you get your act right and punch the necessary buttons, you will definitely influence even the hardest of hearts.

3.   Know the Right Timing: You can't just go all Barrack Obama on people at their most emotional moments. You might end up receiving a punch on the face if you try that. The timing is really important whenever you want to influence the decisions of the people around you. This is, in fact, the best way to make persuasion work. Focus on the timing, know when to strike, and the rest will be history. It's all about the timing with persuasion. When we are sure of the timing, you will be able to move even the hardest of hearts.

General Rule

4. Leveraging Reciprocation: There is a popular saying that goes like this; one good turn deserves another. When you are extremely and selflessly good toward another person, then that person will feel obliged to return the favor in time, no matter how long it may take. The one good you have done will be outlined and stored in the heart of that person. This is just how we are being configured.

Now, how about making good use of this advantage? How about turning this long chain of gratitude to your own benefit? You can help someone out today and use that opportunity of reciprocation to collect a bigger return afterward. They would gladly give you a helping hand knowing fully well that they would also get help back from you in the future when the need arises. The chain goes on and on.

5. Persistence is the Key: When you know what you want, then the best way to go about it is to keep being persistent about it until you make a breakthrough. When you constantly stay glued to your persuasion skills, others are more likely to give in and start seeing things from your point of view. One of the key attributes that must be possessed by someone who possesses the power of persuasion is continuous persistence.

This is the key ingredient of every leader out there in the world. They would stay glued to their beliefs and opinions until their message is passed to every corner of their region. Be like these leaders in order to be persuasive. Abraham Lincoln still remained resolute to his beliefs even after losing lots of elections and the people he held dear. Even to the point of his assassination, he never swayed away from his beliefs. Now, that is real persuasion.

6. Set Your Goals and Expectations: The power of persuasion also deals with making other people believe and trust you no matter how the situation can be. If you can persuade them, then you are obviously asking them to take a chance in your well-set goals and expectations. At the end of the day, if you deliver, then the persuasion power comes in handy. But in cases where you fail to meet these expectations, then you can just start persuading all over again.

7. The Assumption in Persuasion is Wrong: Assumption is a key enemy to persuasion. When we start assuming things, then we fail to see the purpose of persuasion as a whole. Instead of assuming, why not allow ourselves just do the needful? Instead of assuming for others, why not let nature take its course?

Personal Skills

8. Flexibility: He or she that is most flexible possesses the power of persuasion. As a matter of fact, children also possess great powers of persuasion with their childish attitudes. For example, when a child wants something badly and wasn't given it, he or she will resort to all forms of tricks in order to get that thing. The child might start crying even without anyone beating him or her. The child might even start pleading or becoming charming just to get it.

Now that is how great men think and react with persuasion. Persuasion is an art - an important one that deals with being flexible. You have to think of more than one way to influence another person. Thus, the more flexible your behavior can be, the better you will be at being persuasive.

9. Be a Good Communicator: Have you ever seen a leader who isn't good with words? Have you ever seen a leader without the command of good communication skills? All leaders possess the power of communication. That is the only way they can reach their followers. Now, when you apply this principle in your own life, lines will definitely fall in place for you. If you cannot reach even the dumbest of people, then you are not cut out for this kind of skill.

10. Be Calm and Collected Always: This is an attribute that works perfectly with leaders. As a leader who possesses the power of persuasion, you need to be extremely calm at all times, especially in times of need. This is the trait which you can use to your own advantage. In times of adversity, always remember to stay calm. In times of troubles, always remember to stay calm. In times of negativity, always stay positive. This will give hope to the people around you.

Every single concept has its own guiding principles. These principles are what would serve as the light that will illuminate the path towards that concept. Trust me - if you can follow these well-proven and well-tested principles to the letter, then you shouldn't worry about losing yourself on the way. The next chapter will focus on the controversies surrounding the negativity of Emotional Intelligence. You won't want to miss it.

Chapter Nine

The Dark Side of Emotional Intelligence

In as much as we have painted Emotional Intelligence white since the beginning of this book, it still doesn't mean that there is no supposed dark side to the subject matter. As a matter of fact, there is nothing in this life that doesn't come with the pros and cons of it. No matter how perfect it might turn out to be, there will always be a negative side to it, no matter how little it might be. This same point applies to Emotional Intelligence.

Over the past few chapters, we have focused our energy on explaining how much importance and benefit one can derive from Emotional Intelligence if only we had learned to master it. Without a doubt, our life would improve with it, our relationships would sail even higher, and our connection with our inner self would see no bounds. But at what expense would we achieve all these? At what expense would we benefit from all these?

When we focus on the benefits one would derive from Emotional Intelligence, we will easily be carried away without taking a second look at the bad side of it, that is, if this bad sides truly exist. If Emotional Intelligence solves our problem of an emotional outbreak, how about the effects it might leave? You won't find a lot of books, Internet materials, and studies that would focus on the negative part of Emotional Intelligence. It is as if they all had reached a consensus of neglecting this crucial part of Emotional Intelligence. If you would want to sell out an idea to the public, wouldn't it be more appropriate if you go out clean?

This chapter will focus its lens on the so-called negative aspects of Emotional Intelligence. It will sensitize you on the negative effects you might encounter on your journey toward being emotionally independent. Don't get it twisted; Emotional Intelligence is a very good thing. Acknowledging it, identifying it, understanding it, and using it to influence the decisions of the people around you is a very good trait we all would want to have. Some won't even mind killing for this power.

However, it comes with a price and this price is what I will delve into. According to a whole lot of people out there, Emotional Intelligence comes with its own blemish. Many have believed the subject matter to be misconstrued. They believe Emotional Intelligence doesn't really have the right basis to be studied either as intelligence or as a personal character. In the same vein, no matter how well we look at this argument, we would only agree that there is no clear demarcation.

While some people have been of the notion that Emotional Intelligence is actually an intelligence, due to the fact that it can be tested and measured, others just believe it is something that can only be gotten as a result of your in-built traits. Now, if the basis of Emotional Intelligence is not even known and established, how can anyone claim to even understand what Emotional Intelligence really entails? Although there had been numerous examples of world leaders that had been able to demonstrate the control of their emotions at it's best, would it be correct if we call that Emotional Intelligence?

The definition and constructiveness of Emotional Intelligence are not well taken according to some group of scholars. They believe Emotional Intelligence doesn't have a clear background as to the measurements and tests. There is a strange contradiction between these distinctions. How well should Emotional Intelligence be measured or tested? Is it as intelligence or as a behavior? It is one thing to exude this trait as intelligence and it is another to project the trait as a behavior. Thus, which one is correct? Quite controversial, isn't it?

Aside from this, many also believed that there are no guiding principles that explain the use of Emotional Intelligence. We had seen or heard of cases where a whole lot of people who had mastered their emotions and even possesses the power of persuasion had used this outstanding trait for the worst things ever. Instead of making good use of this amazing skill or trait into making the world a better place, they had abused it instead by using it to achieve their selfish aim.

Adolf Hitler is a very good example of this selfish use of Emotional Intelligence. Now the question is, how do we stop people from misusing this trait? Are there even any guiding values and principles surrounding the use of Emotional Intelligence? Believe it or not, in as much as many people believe that Emotional Intelligence does more good than harm, others are forced to believe otherwise. Thus, there is a controversial tussle between both thoughts as to which is actually correct.

If you judge these notions by their various points, you would agree with me that both of them are actually correct. Furthermore, there is no clear distinction as to what kind of behaviors or intelligence patterns are familiar with Emotional Intelligence. Although there have been ongoing studies that would shed more light on this aspect, one can still say there aren't enough yardsticks that can be used in showing one's emotional capabilities.

Emotional Intelligence is just about throwing unreasonable feat about controlling one's emotions or outcomes. The controversial belief that this utopian idea is possible should not be conceived by anyone. Many religious leaders would agree with this notion. They would tell you being emotional is a feeling that comes with our being. It is how we are being configured. If Eve wasn't emotional, we wouldn't be down here on earth. If Cain hadn't been emotional, we wouldn't have known sin.

This is from the religious point of view. Instead of us trying hard to perfect the mysteries of God, how about we just enjoy it and let it flow? It is only robots that can't possess emotions or feelings. Instead of depriving yourself of these feelings as they come, how about allowing them to manifest on their own? Additionally, many people believed that Emotional Intelligence gained momentum in recent years solely because of their social capabilities and not their scientific or emotional control.

The world today is going wide and wild, thus, there is a need for people to possesses the power to control and understand the emotions of others around them, not because of anything but because of living together in harmony. Now, with the recent development and technological advancement like the nuclear, atomic, and biological weapons that are possessed by various nations, there is a need for Emotional Intelligence. In order words, the world doesn't need Emotional Intelligence because of its so-called tenets and principles but because of order and harmony.

But how sure are we that this trait would be the rise of a new Hitler? In another controversial opinion, many believed that Emotional Intelligence is a cover-up for the exploitation and capitalization of the world by the world capitalist giants out there. In order to make the exploited feel better and to continue exploiting labor and the resources available for all, Emotional Intelligence was projected to put the mind of the people at ease.

If the people that are supposed to be revolting are busy finding new ways to build, repair, and reconstruct old and new connections with family and friends, then that would sway their minds off any form of revolt. Thus, the world capitalist system would now begin to look more caring, compassionate, and attentive to the problems of the masses. This is just another strategy which many believe would begin to fail sooner or later.

Now, there are two things involved with this so-called Emotional Intelligence. It's either Emotional Intelligence is the secret recipe that would make man extremely happy or it's the same old garbage that is just well repackaged in another form. In as much as many believed Emotional Intelligence goes in line with the former, others just believe Emotional Intelligence is nothing but the reincarnation of previous ideas that had refused to work in the past. Thus, it's only a matter of time before it fails.

Additionally, the control of one's emotions can be quite a curse more than a blessing. How? I'll tell you. When we are at the center of our emotions, when we know our left from right even at our weakest moments, and when we take control of our emotions no matter the circumstances or situation, we will be able to shield ourselves from making mistakes or even allowing our emotions control our decision-making skills. Now, this is a good thing.

But the curse comes when we now start developing the understanding of the feelings of others. We would be forced to act selfishly sometimes by using this trait to influence the decisions of others. Even if these decisions are great so long it doesn't favor us, we would still think of influencing the decisions. When this happens, we would realize that we have been making others do our bidding while neglecting theirs. We would find out we have been using our outstanding trait to exert an influence in the lives of others at the expense of their happiness. Now, this is a curse.

Also, there is no fine line between persuasion and manipulation. There is no fine line between influencing and brainwashing. Emotional Intelligence can be greatly misconstrued with respect to this definition. Now, if Emotional Intelligence can be misconceived this way, would you have said Emotional Intelligence is a good thing? Would you have vouched for the importance of this trait? Thus, there is no demarcation on how to properly wield the power of Emotional Intelligence.

While some people just believe persistence is the key to persuasion as regards Emotional Intelligence, others just believe Emotional Intelligence can be easily tainted with manipulation and brainwashing. If the tactics of persuasion don't work, they would just switch to force and manipulation. This is very evident in the world today. Little wonder why there are lots of brainwashed people around today. Persuasion deals with being intelligent and flexible, while manipulation deals with being rigid.

Others are also of the thought that Emotional Intelligence doesn't have anything to do with morality. As a matter of fact, it is very different from the realm of morality. No matter how hard you twist it, Morality and Emotional Intelligence are two diverse concepts which shouldn't be put together as two sides of the same coin.

When you are guided by the principles of morality, then you are able to define your Emotional Intelligence even better. But if you are not, you might easily get carried away by this outstanding trait, thereby, misusing its powers for your own selfish gain. Misguiding and motivating people wrongly would now be the best friend. This is where a lot of people with Emotional Intelligence end of being corrupt in the end. Without morality in it, one is bound to be corrupt.

This had been the major argument and believed to be the darkest side of Emotional Intelligence. If Emotional Intelligence can be guided, if Emotional Intelligence has it's own set of rules and regulations, if the use or Emotional Intelligence can be monitored or measured, and if the use of Emotional Intelligence can be greatly used, then there is nothing to be scared of. Emotional Intelligence would just be one hell of a powerful tool in reaching for greatness. Be that as it may, it is still as effective and efficient as ever even with its dark side. Thus, when used wrongly, Emotional Intelligence can be the most dangerous tool in the world.

The ability to control the feelings and decisions of others by being persuasive can be the most dangerous weapon one might need in order to reach the peak. This is why people of sound and great minds are being advised to only go into Emotional Intelligence. Whether we like it or not, we still can't stop anybody from harnessing this power. Remember, with great power comes great responsibility. But the question here is how can we be certain that the person wielding the power of Emotional Intelligence is of great mind? What if the persons are shallow thinkers that only see things their way?

Emotional Intelligence goes in line with being empathetic towards the feelings of others. According to Emotional Intelligence, when you show care for others in their moment of need, you are certainly building a pathway for yourself into that person's life. Thus, what is the assurance that our care and support we show to the people around us isn't just for our own selfish desire? Aside from this, the term manipulation and persuasion can be greatly misconstrued.

What is the assurance that you are being persuasive when in the real sense of the world, all your tactics are pointing towards manipulation? Additionally, people only make the word persuasion in order to paint their work as a good thing. And others might also tag you as a manipulator when they want people to think your work involves something bad. The bottom line is that people now use both words to suit themselves and give their explanations meaning. Even if you are good at persuasion, they would call you a manipulator if they don't like you and if you are a manipulator and extremely good at what you do, people won't see you for what you truly are.

Be that as it may, there is no such thing as purity without a blemish except the extraordinary. In as much as these controversies aren't really wrong, we can still call them the dark sides to Emotional Intelligence. Now, that doesn't mean Emotional Intelligence is totally bad. If you can control yourself and discipline your mind towards the thought of a greater good, then Emotional Intelligence is meant for you.

Chapter Ten

Does Emotional Intelligence Really Exist? (Now you know better)

I believe you know better as regards Emotional Intelligence, especially as we have discussed everything that you need to know about the subject matter. Many people still believe Emotional Intelligence does not really exist. Instead, they are of the opinion that our emotions are something we can't control, no matter how hard we try. Now, this is one place they always get it wrong. Emotional Intelligence does not refer to the control of our emotions directly but rather the control of the outcome as regards these emotions.

In other words, we can only hold control of our emotions via our own actions. If we end up holding our emotions intact without letting it influence our decisions, then we can say that we are being emotionally intelligent. Have you ever wondered why some people just act so mature no matter the circumstances? It is true that the older we get, the more we see life in a different dimension, however, not every old person has this ability and not every young person lacks it.

When you show everyone around you constantly how to be a better person, no matter the circumstances, then you are definitely exhibiting the traits of Emotional Intelligence. Just like the saying goes, leaders aren't born, they are made - and so is Emotional intelligence in the real sense of the world. Many believe this ability is not something you are born with. Normally, an average human being is filled with all sorts of emotions running through the body.

From the regular emotions down to the crazy ones, each emotion depicts the feelings that are all boxed up inside the body. Now, nobody without the appropriate training or discipline can choose to forgo these emotions as they erupt out of us. In a situation where our emotions might take the better part of us, someone who is a master of their emotions would definitely react calmly and maturely. They would definitely use their heads ahead of their hearts.

In a situation where a diligent and hardworking employee just got sacked, a normal person would get extremely mad over the unfair treatment. No matter the excuse given by the organization, be it recession, retrenchment, or even resizing of their staff strength, you just won't get the drift. Your emotions would definitely get the better part of you. You would be forced to accept reality in the long run. But before then, you might have become a shadow of yourself.

A lot of people would fall back into their shell. They would go into acute depression, thereby, shutting everybody out. To them, it would be like the whole world has gathered together just to be against them. When this happens, it would take the grace of God for us to be able to snap out of this mood sucking moments. Now, the question I would ask is this, why make yourself suffer by going through these particular kinds of torture? Why go through these heartbreaking moments when all you need to do is just to reconcile with the situation and make sure you stop letting your emotions take control?

Trust me, when we do this, our spiritual level will shoot up. Our relationships would thrive and see the new light. Our emotions would be tolerated even further. Our life would start taking good shape. Additionally, Emotional Intelligence goes in line with a perfect and sound body. Your body should be in a good working condition. That is the only way you can think with your head and instead of your heart. That is the only way you can keep your emotions in check.

I made an example with my own dad above as regards this point. An ailing body is a vulnerable one. When one gets sick and the body starts paving way for different kinds of illness, our emotions tend to get the better part of us. That is when we are most vulnerable. When my dad fell really sick, the same thing happened to him. He would easily snap at anyone in the room with him at the slightest mistake. He would get tensed at everything, no matter how little.

Like the master of Emotional Intelligence that I am, I already knew what to expect from the old man. I knew I had to be extra careful each time I was around him, but my siblings didn't know this and they became the victim of my father's emotional outbreaks. Now, after reading the chapters of this amazing book, would you really still come out boldly to say that Emotional Intelligence is just a myth? That it is just a fallacy?

Be that as it may, some people are of the opinion that the need for Emotional Intelligence is very crucial, especially with the rising societal issues that have sprung up in recent times. They believe Emotional Intelligence exists because of the solution it would proffer to these societal problems. If people can be more accommodating toward the emotions of others, and if we are also able to control our own emotions or the outcomes, as the case may be, then we will be able to move forward as one society.

That is an amazing concept of Emotional Intelligence. This explains why a lot of people don't mind paying large sums of money toward training themselves for a better version of themselves. What Emotional Intelligence does is to metamorphose someone from weak to strong, from needy to needed, and from average to intelligent. It would help develop your emotional skills and transform you from the average person you were yesterday to the intelligent person you will be later.

Others believe Emotional Intelligence does not really exist in the real sense because of its inability to be measured or even curtailed to an extent. There is absolutely no true measure or test of Emotional Intelligence rather than the fact that you stay neutral to the tribulations you find yourself in. Many believe that alone doesn't make you truly intelligent emotionally. Everybody can fake a nonchalant attitude to their emotions if the need arises. As desperate times call for desperate measures, so does this particular subject matter can be applied given the peculiarity of the situation. Thus, there is no big deal about it.

No matter how we turn this point, there is an atom of truth in it. If we can't truly come out to say we can measure this intelligence, then a mediocre person can come out today and start claiming the trait. Aside from this, I believe if you can say someone is intelligent in a particular field (mathematically, psychologically, sportsmanship, and so much more), so can you say someone who can perfectly control the outcome of their emotions is emotionally intelligent.

If a person is intelligent mathematically, that person would definitely excel in mathematics. Any questions bade of mathematics that are thrown toward him would be like throwing eggs on rocks. He would definitely solve them with no issues at all. This same instance applies to Emotional Intelligence. If one is emotionally intelligent, then he or she would definitely triumph in life. When life throws him or her different tribulations and obstacles, he or she will be able to sail past them swiftly and smoothly. In every sphere of life, an emotionally unintelligent person would definitely suffer as his or her emotions would lead the way each time in his or her affairs.

Finally, this argument has been going on for at least a decade with a lot of people rallying around both notions. If Emotional Intelligence really does exist, then does that mean every average person that can control their emotions or even fake it is emotionally intelligent? And if it doesn't exist, does that mean every leader out there that had been able to reach a lot of followers faked their Emotional Intelligence? If you can answer these questions correctly, then you should be able to tell if it exists or not.

Conclusion

I must say this had been one hell of a journey. From the beginning of this amazing book to the end, it had been an interesting journey which will definitely leave a mark in us. If you didn't know about Emotional Intelligence, well now you know better. Now you can do things in a much better form than the way you had done them before. Now you can approach things differently (calm and collected), unlike the way you had approached them before (emotional).

Without a doubt, I believe you now have a potential of managing and holding on to your old and new relationships. Nothing beats someone who has the whole world in his or her pockets. Now, how does one possesses that power? It's through Emotional Intelligence! When you have the power to turn every tide around and use them for your own benefit, people will always wonder if you are even human at all.

Remember, with great power comes great responsibility. Do not in any way misuse this outstanding power to manipulate or oppress anyone. What Emotional Intelligence teaches is to be compassionate and think of the greater good first. If you feel your relationships and connections are fading away, you know what to do. Instead of going back to your shell until someone fortunately comes along the line to build you back up, how about you check inward for a solution.

This is where unveiling your true and inner self comes into the picture. No one knows you better than yourself. Always make good use of this rare gift. Connect with your true self with the help of Spirituality. Go on a journey of discovering yourself and that will help you come back even stronger. Hold your values and principles tight. They would serve as the torch that would illuminate your path when you seem lost in your journey towards discovering yourself.

Now, go out there and make a difference. Go out there and show the world how much of the garbage you can take without flinching. As the saying goes, when life throws you a lemon, then make lemonade out of it. Any situation or circumstances you find yourself in, staying calm is of the essence. That would make you think ahead, and fast. You would be shocked at where the panacea would come from. Sometimes, it is our inability to be calm during tribulations that make us unable to see how close the solutions to the problems are.

Be that as it may, Emotional Intelligence can only be possible with the help of the 3Ps; patience, perseverance, and persuasion. If you can easily wield these three key weapons, then the rest will be history. You will be shocked at how great you would be, from your place of work to your home. Everything will fall into place. When your bosses start favoring you, others might think it's a fluke, not knowing its Emotional Intelligence that is working well for you.

Now, be the good person you have always been. Don't let this great power get to your head. And remember, absolutely power corrupts absolutely. Thanks for sticking with us all through our journey. You've been amazing. God bless and be Emotional Intelligent!

www.ingramcontent.com/pod-product-compliance
Lightning Source LLC
Chambersburg PA
CBHW071448080526
44587CB00014B/2040